THE VICE PRESIDENCY OF THE UNITED STATES: EVOLUTION OF THE MODERN OFFICE

THE VICE PRESIDENCY OF THE UNITED STATES: EVOLUTION OF THE MODERN OFFICE

HAROLD C. RELYEA AND CHARLES V. ARJA

Nova Science Publishers, Inc.
New York

Senior Editors: Susan Boriotti and Donna Dennis
Coordinating Editor: Tatiana Shohov
Office Manager: Annette Hellinger
Graphics: Wanda Serrano
Book Production: Matthew Kozlowski, Jonathan Rose and Jennifer Vogt
Circulation: Raymond Davis, Cathy DeGregory, Ave Maria Gonzalez and Andre Tillman
Communications and Acquisitions: Serge P. Shohov

Library of Congress Cataloging-in-Publication Data

Relyea, Harold.
    The vice presidency of the United States: evolution of the modern office / Harold C. Relyea
and Charles V. Arja.
        p. cm.
    Includes Index.
    ISBN 1-59033-106-0
        1. Vice Presidents—United States—History. 2. United States—Politics and government.
    I. Arja, Charles V. II. Title.

    JK609.5 .R45 2001
    973'.09'9—dc21

                                                            2001054669

Copyright ©2002 by Nova Science Publishers, Inc.
                227 Main Street, Suite 100
                Huntington, New York 11743
                Tele. 631-424-6682   Fax 631-424-4666
                e-mail: Novascience@earthlink.net
                Web Site: http://www.nexusworld.com/nova

Printed in the United States of America

CONTENTS

PREFACE

Something of an afterthought, the vice presidential office came to the attention of the delegates to the constitutional convention in the closing days of their deliberations in 1787. The Vice President's constitutional mandate vested him with two responsibilities: presiding over the deliberations of the Senate and standing by to succeed the President in the event of his death. Although some Vice Presidents informally gave the President advice, the inclusion of the Vice President in Cabinet deliberations did not occur until the second decade of the twentieth century. Woodrow Wilson set the precedent by requiring his Vice President to preside over a few Cabinet meetings while Wilson was in France negotiating the Treaty of Versailles. Thereafter, future presidents continued this practice, with Franklin D. Roosevelt making the most use of his Vice President, launching the modern version of this office. This book reviews the evolution of the modern vice presidency -- the historical events and developments that have contributed to the expansion of the office beyond its largely legislative branch character to include diverse and important executive branch duties. Each Vice President is briefly discussed along with interesting facts about them.

Chapter 1

PRESIDENTIAL AND VICE PRESIDENTIAL TERMS AND TENURE

Thomas H. Neale

ABSTRACT

Presidential and vice presidential terms and tenure are governed by Article II, Section 1 of the Constitution, and the 20th and 22nd Amendments to the Constitution. Article II prescribes a four-year term. Section 1 of the 20th Amendment provides that terms of office for the President and Vice President end at 12:00 noon on January 20th of each year following a presidential election. From 1789 through 1940, chief executives adhered to a self-imposed omit of two terms. That precedent was broken by President Franklin D. Roosevelt, who was elected four times (1932, 1936, 1940, and 1944). The 22nd Amendment, proposed and ratified following the Roosevelt presidency, provides that "No person shall be elected to the office of the President more than twice..." Further, Vice Presidents who succeed to the presidency can be elected to two full terms as President if they have served less than two years of their predecessor's term (up to 10 years of service). If they have served more than two years of their predecessor's term (up to 10 years of service). If they have served more than two years of a predecessor's term they can be elected to only one additional term (between four and eight years of service, depending on when the Vice President succeeded to the presidency). It is unclear whether a two-term President could succeed to the presidency from the vice presidency or some other office in line of succession; experts disagree on whether this would be constitutional. Proposals for change have included both repeal of the 22nd Amendment and the two-term limitation, and substitution of a single six-year term for the President.

TERMS AND TENURE IN THE CONSTITUTION

The question of presidential term length and re-eligibility were the subject of considerable discussion at the 1787 Constitutional Convention. The convention faced two basic tenure issues: duration of the President's term, and whether incumbents would be able to serve multiple terms (re-eligibility). The delegates sought to balance the need for energy and stability in the executive (thus suggesting a term longer than the one or two years served by most state governors at the time), with the fear that a too-lengthy term would lead to excessive concentration of power. The question of re-eligibility was similarly influenced by fears of tyranny: would an infinitely re-electible presidency lead to dictatorship or monarchy? This issue was further complicated by the fact that most delegates expected the President to be chosen by Congress. If he were, and were also re-eligible, they feared the incumbent would spend much of his time and energy in schemes to ensure reelection, and that this would negatively affect the goal of separation of powers and checks and balances among the branches of government. Would the executive become too dependent on Congress?

Two early drafts of the Constitution (the Virginia and New Jersey plans) specified that the federal executive would be elected by Congress and eligible to serve just one term, but neither suggested what length the term should be. The delegates initially approved a single seven-year term, with no prospect for reelection. They later changed the term to six years, and dropped the prohibition against additional service, but restored the seven-year term, without re-eligibility, after further debate. This interim decision was ultimately superseded late in the convention, when the Committee on Unfinished Business submitted a report that provided for a four-year term, with unlimited re-eligibility. The committee also addressed the question of executive independence by vesting the President's election in a group of electors chosen in the states, the Electoral College.[1] Opponents sought unsuccessfully to reinstate the single term requirement, but the final version,

---

[1] For additional information on the Electoral College, see CRS Report RS20273, *The Electoral College: How It Works in Contemporary Presidential Elections.*

as approved by the convention, states the familiar formula found in Article II, Section I of the Constitution:

> The executive Power shall be vested in a President of the United States of America. He shall hold his Office during the Term of four Years, and, together with the Vice President, chosen for the same Term, be elected, as follows...[2]

THE TWO-TERM TRADITION

From early 19th century through Franklin Roosevelt's 1940 decision to run for an unprecedented third term, American Presidents considered themselves bound by a tradition that they should serve no more than two terms. Although Washington is credited with establishing this tradition, his 1796 Farewell Address made no mention of any such constitutional precedent: "...every day the increasing weight of years admonishes me more and more that the shade of retirement is as necessary to me as it will be welcome."[3] According to modern scholars, the two-term tradition is more properly attributed to Thomas Jefferson, who expressed concern about "perpetual re-eligibility" in the presidency as early as 1788.[4] Petitioned to run for a third term in 1807, Jefferson declined, stating his belief that, "If some termination to the services of the chief Magistrate be not fixed by the Constitution, or supplied by practice, his office, nominally four years, will in fact become for life...I should unwillingly be the person who, disregarding the sound precedent set by an illustrious predecessor [Washington], should furnish the first example of prolongation beyond the second term of office."[5]

The two-term limit quickly acquired the force of tradition. Three of Jefferson's four immediate successors, James Madison, James Monroe, and Andrew Jackson, stepped down at the close of their second terms, while the fourth, John Quincy Adams, was defeated for reelection. In fact, historian

---

[2] For detailed discussions of the presidency at the Constitutional Convention, see: Thomas E. Cronin, ed., *Inventing the American Presidency* (Lawrence, KS: U. of Kansas Press, 1989) or Charles Coleman Thach, *The Creation of the Presidency, 1775-1789: A Study in Constitutional History* (Baltimore: John Hopkins U. Press, 1922).

[3] "Washington's Farewell Address," in Henry Steele Commager, ed., *Documents of American History*, 9th ed. (Englewood Cliffs, NJ: Prentice-Hall, 1973), p. 170.

[4] Michael Nelson, ed., *Guide to the Presidency*, 2nd ed. (Washington: Congressional Quarterly, 1996), p. 59.

Michael Nelson notes that, during the second quarter of the 19th century, the Whig Party (and many Democrats) supported a one-term limit, and suggests that this proposal may have influenced presidential tenure for a quarter century following Jackson's retirement in 1837, during which period no President served more than a single term.[6] Abraham Lincoln was the first President since Jackson to be elected to a second term (in 1864). In the 68 years between the death of Lincoln in 1865, and the inauguration of Franklin D. Roosevelt in 1933, only Ulysses Grant and Woodrow Wilson served two consecutive terms, while Grover Cleveland was defeated for reelection in 1888, but was reelected to a second, non-consecutive, term in 1892. During this long period, only Grant explored the possibility of a third term, in 1880, while Theodore Roosevelt declined to run in 1908, notwithstanding his considerable popularity.[7]

The two-term mold was broken by President Franklin D. Roosevelt in 1940. Following his 1936 reelection, it was widely assumed that Roosevelt would step down at the end of his second term. In 1939, however, the political landscape was transformed by the outbreak of World War II. As the conflict erupted into a world crisis in the spring and summer of 1940, Roosevelt, after a long silence on the subject, let it be known that he would accept the Democratic Party nomination for a third term, if it were offered. The party obliged with considerable enthusiasm, and the President was reelected for a third term that November. With the United States deeply involved in the war by 1944, the injunction not to "change horses in the middle of the stream" seemed even more compelling, and Roosevelt, although in failing health, was elected a fourth time.

---

[5] Quoted in ibid., p. 49.

[6] Ibid., pp. 49-50. It is, however, arguable that electoral defeat (Martin Van Buren), death in office (William Henry Harrison, Zachary Taylor), and generally recognized failure in office (Franklin Pierce, James Buchanan) contributed as much, or more, to the single-term presidencies of the period.

[7] Grant found Republican leaders opposed to a third term. Although Roosevelt had been elected President only once, he had served all but six months of William McKinley's second term, to which he had succeeded as Vice President.

THE 20TH AMENDMENT: BEGINNING PRESIDENTIAL TERMS ON JANUARY 20

From 1789 through 1937, presidential and vice presidential terms ended on March 4 of every year following a presidential election, a date set by the Second Congress.[8] This arrangement led to a four-month interval between presidential elections (held in November) and inaugurations (held on March 4 of the following year).[9] Section 1 of the 20th Amendment, proposed by Congress in 1932, and ratified by the states in 1933, changed the date for presidential terms to January 20 (effective 1937), and that of Congress to January 3 (effective in 1935). The amendment was the culmination of a long campaign to shorten the interval between election and inauguration, eliminate lame duck sessions of Congress, and ensure that a newly elected Congress would count electoral votes and conduct contingent election of the President and Vice President, if necessary.[10] Since 1937, Presidents have been inaugurated on January 20, except when the day falls on a Sunday; in such cases, the President is customarily sworn in at a private White House ceremony on the 20th; and the public ceremony is held the next day.

THE 22ND AMENDMENT: TERM LIMITS FOR THE PRESIDENT

The 22nd Amendment, which effectively limits Presidents to two terms in office, has frequently been described as a reaction to the presidency of Franklin Roosevelt.[11] The Amendment was a top priority for the 80th Congress (1947-1948), the first to be controlled by Republicans since 1931. Debate on

---

[8] March 4 was selected in 1788 under the Articles of Confederation, when Congress voted that "the first Wednesday in March next be the time" at which the term of the First Congress would begin, a day that fell on March 4 in 1789. The Second Congress confirmed the date and extended it to presidential terms in 1792 (1 Stat. 241).

[9] During this period, retiring or defeated Presidents were considered to be political cripples, "lame ducks." At the same time, the second "lame duck" session of a Congress followed congressional elections, leaving a House and Senate that included retiring or repudiated Members to legislate for several months *after* the election.

[10] For additional information on contingent election, see CRS Report RS20300, *Election of the President and Vice President by Congress: Contingent Election.*

[11] Alan P. Grimes, *Democracy and the Amendments to the Constitution,* (Lexington, MA: D.C. Heath, 1978), pp. 114-116. Thomas E. Cronin, "Twenty-Second Amendment," in *Encyclopedia of the American Presidency*, Leonard W. Levy and Louis Fisher, eds. (New York: Simon and Schuster, 1994), vol. 4, pp. 1511-1512.

the proposal was the occasion of considerable rancor, as some Democrats claimed it was both undemocratic and an act of posthumous revenge against Roosevelt, while Republicans argued their goal was the prevention of excess concentration of power in the hands of one person. The idea of term limits was not new, however; one scholar notes that 270 amendments to limit presidential tenure had been proposed prior to 1947. Moreover, the measure passed both houses by wide margins, and with some degree of Democratic support.[12] The Amendment states that, "No person shall be elected to the office of the President more than twice..." It also provides (in an amendment offered by Senator Robert A. Taft) for Vice Presidents who succeed to the office: they can be elected to two full terms as President if they serve less than two years of their predecessor's term (up to 10 years of service). If they have served more than two years of the term to which they succeed, they can be elected to only one additional term (between four and eight years of service, depending on when the Vice President succeeded to the presidency).[13] The Amendment also specifically exempted "any person holding the office of President when this article was proposed..." that is, incumbent President Harry Truman. Proposed in 1947, the Amendment was declared ratified on March 1, 1951, after being approved by 36 states.

Since its ratification, the 22nd Amendment has applied to three Presidents who served two full terms: Dwight Eisenhower (1953-1961), Ronald Reagan (1981-1989), and William Clinton (1993-2001). Of the remaining chief executives, John Kennedy (1961-1963) died in office; Lyndon Johnson (1963-1969) declined to run for a second full term; Richard Nixon (1969-1974) resigned from office; and Gerald Ford (1974-1977), James Carter (1977-1981), and George H. W. Bush (1989-1993) were defeated in reelection bids.

---

[12] Cronin, "Twenty-Second Amendment," p. 1511. Fifty Democrats voted with Republicans in the House (March 21, 1947), for a margin of 285 to 121 in support of the measure. In the Senate, 16 Democrats contributed to the winning margin of 59 to 23 (March 12, 1947). Grimes, *Democracy and the Amendments to the Constitution*, pp. 119-120.

[13] For example, Lyndon Johnson became President in November 1963, 34 months into the term to which he and John Kennedy were elected. Since he served less than two years of this term, he could have been elected to two full terms. Conversely, Gerald Ford became President in August 1974, 19 months into Richard Nixon's second term. Since Ford served more than two years of Nixon's term, he could have been elected to only one full term.

Is the 22nd Amendment an Absolute Term Limitation?

The 22nd Amendment prohibits anyone from being elected President more than twice, but could a President who was elected to two terms as chief executive be subsequently elected Vice President, and then succeed to the presidency on the incumbent's death, resignation, or removal from office? This issue was raised during discussions of the 22nd Amendment in 1960, when President Eisenhower was about to become the first President affected by the amendment; while it has received little attention since, the question remains open.[14] Some argue that the 12th Amendment statement that "...no person constitutionally ineligible to the office of President shall be eligible to that of Vice-President..." *ipso facto* bars any term-limited President from serving as Vice President, or succeeding to the presidency from any other line-of-succession position (the Speaker of the House, the President pro tempore of the Senate, the Cabinet, etc.).[15] Others maintain that the 12th Amendment's qualifications arguably apply only to the standard requirements of age, residence, and "natural-born citizenship." The 22nd Amendment's prohibition, they suggest, can be interpreted as extending only to eligibility for *election*, not *service*; thus, a term-limited President could be elected Vice President, and then succeed to the presidency to serve the balance of his successor's term (he would not, however, be eligible to run for *election* to an additional term).[16] It seems likely that this question will be answered conclusively barring an actual occurrence of the hypothesis developed above. As former Secretary of State Dean Acheson commented when the issue was discussed in 1960, it may be "more unlikely than unconstitutional."[17]

---

[14] Stephen W. Stathis, "The Twenty-Second Amendment: A Practical Remedy or Partisan Maneuver?" *Constitutional Commentary*, vol. 7, winter 1990, pp. 76-77.

[15] Henry H. Fowler, quoted in Robert E. Clark, "The Constitutional Issues: A 'Back-door' Third Term?" *The Sunday Star* (Washington, DC), Jan. 31, 1960, p. C-4.

[16] Edward S. Corwin, quoted in ibid.; Johnny H. Killian, CRS Senior Specialist in Public Law, conversation of Feb. 8, 2001.

[17] George Dixon, "Washington Scene...Ike's Right to V.P. Spot," *The Washington Post*, Jan. 21, 1960, p. A-23.

PROPOSALS FOR CHANGE

Repeal of the 22nd Amendment

Proposals for repeal of the 22nd Amendment have been advanced on several occasions since its ratification. These proposals have usually been offered during the second term of a President who has enjoyed a degree of success or popularity. Advocates of repeal assert that a popular or successful two-term President should be able to serve additional terms, that the limit imposed by the 22nd Amendment prevents the voters from choosing the President they prefer, and that reelection is the ultimate term limit mechanism. Supporters of presidential term limits argue that eight years is enough time in such a powerful office, and that longer presidential tenure could result in excessive concentration of power in the executive. Examples of related proposals include H.J. Res. 690, 99th Congress (Representative Dornan); H.J. Res. 156, 100th Congress (Representative Vander Jagt); and H.J. Res. 17 (Representative Serrano), H.J. 24 (Representative Frank), and H.J. Res. 38 (Representative Hoyer with Representatives Hyde, Frank, Berman, Sensenbrenner, Sabo, and Pallone), all introduced in the 106th Congresses; and, H.J. Res. 4 (Representative Serrano) in the 107th Congress. None of these proposals received any action beyond pro forma committee referral. Proposals in the 99th and 100th Congress were referred to the House Judiciary Committee's Subcommittee on Civil and Constitutional Rights, now the Subcommittee on the Constitution.

Six-Year Presidential Term

Another option for change that has received occasional attention is the six-year term for the President and Vice President, usually coupled with provisions limiting these officers to a single term. Proponents of this reform assert that the six-year term would free the President from partisan political concerns associated with campaigning for reelection, thus allowing the chief executive to concentrate on public policy issues. Further, decisions on these questions would less likely be judged by their impact on the President's reelection prospects. Finally, advocates suggest that a single term would eliminate the "lame duck" diminution of power and influence experienced by some Presidents during their last years in office. Opponents counter by asserting that a single six-year term would make an oncoming chief executive who has no prospect for reelection a lame duck the day he entered office. Lack of the prospect of reelection, they contend, would actually reduce a President's accountability. The single term provision is undemocratic and would deprive the nation of the services of a capable chief executive. Further, they argue that a six-year term is too long for a failed President, and too short for a successful one: "Six years for an incompetent, erratic, or listless President would have been disastrous on several past occasions, and could be again."[18] The most recent six-year term proposals were offered in the 101st Congress (1989-1991), including H.J. Res. 6 (Representative Brooks), H.J. Res. 52 (Representative Frenzel), and H.J. Res. 176 (Representative Guarini). No action, other than *pro forma* referral to the then-Subcommittee on Monopolies and Commercial Law of the House Judiciary Committee was taken on any of these proposals.

---

[18] James L. Sundquist, "Six-Year Presidential Term," in *Encyclopedia of the American Presidency*, vol. 4, p. 1375.

Chapter 2

THE VICE PRESIDENCY OF THE UNITED STATES: EVOLUTION OF THE MODERN OFFICE

Harold C. Relyea

Something of an afterthought, the vice presidential office came to the attention of the delegates to the constitutional convention in the closing days of their deliberations in 1787. The Vice President's constitutional mandate vested him with two responsibilities: presiding over the deliberations of the Senate and standing by to succeed to the presidency in the event of the incumbent's death. For the next 140 years, those holding the vice presidential office served only these functions. Indeed, the Vice President soon came to be regarded as a legislative branch official. However, for six incumbents during this period, their service was particularly important to the nation when they succeeded to the presidency. They included John Tyler, Millard Fillmore, Andrew Johnson, Chester A. Arthur, Theodore Roosevelt, and Calvin Coolidge.

Although some Vice Presidents informally provided advice to the Presidents with whom they served, the inclusion of the Vice President in Cabinet deliberations did not occur until the second decade of the 20th century. Consequently, Cabinet members usually were more and better informed about the policies and practices of an administration than the man who might be required to lead that administration in the event of the President's death. Woodrow Wilson fractured the precedent in 1919 when he requested Vice President Thomas R. Marshall to preside over a few Cabinet meetings while he was in France negotiating the treaty of peace concluding World War I. Thereafter, President Warren G. Harding regularly included Vice President Calvin Coolidge in Cabinet sessions. Elected to the presidency in 1924, Coolidge invited Vice President Charles G. Dawes to Cabinet meetings, but he declined. During the tenure of Herbert C. Hoover, Vice President Charles Curtis only occasionally attended Cabinet deliberations. With the presidency of Franklin Roosevelt, however, the practice of including the Vice President in the Cabinet became tradition. Moreover, President Roosevelt began to make other uses of Vice President John N. Garner as an arm of the presidency, launching the modern version of this office.[1]

EXPANDED RESPONSIBILITIES

During the latter half of the 19th century, broader thinking about other roles the Vice President might play began to be evidenced. When Congress chartered the Smithsonian Institution in 1846, the Vice President was statutorily designated a member of its Board of Regents.[2] Various editions of the Congressional Directory, the official almanac of Congress, reveal that James S. Sherman served as chairman of the congressional Commission on Enlarging the Capitol Grounds in 1911; Thomas R. Marshall was a member of the Arlington Memorial Bridge Commission from 1914 to 1921, succeeded by Calvin Coolidge during 1921-1923, Charles G. Dawes during 1925-1929, Charles Curtis during 1929-1933, and John N. Garner during the final months of 1933. Similarly, Dawes became a member of the congressional Commission on Enlarging the Capitol Grounds in 1925, and was succeeded by Curtis, who chaired the panel, and Garner, who also chaired. In addition, beginning in 1925, Dawes, Curtis, and Garner were successively ex officio members of the Commission for the Celebration of the 200th Anniversary of the Birth of George Washington.

---

[1] Appendix 1 of this report identifies those individuals who held the position of Vice President and the Presidents with whom they served.
[2] 9 Stat. 102.

JOHN N. GARNER

A veteran of the legislature, John N. Garner came to the vice presidency on March 4, 1933, when he was 64 years old. A lawyer by training, he served as a judge in Uvalde County, Texas, during 1893-1896; moved on to the Texas House of Representatives in 1898; and then to the U.S. House of Representatives in 1903, where he served for the next 30 years. He was chosen House minority leader in 1928, and was elected Speaker in 1931. A life-long Democrat, Garner has been described as a Jeffersonian, a man who thought that "we have too many laws," and who believed in limited government – confined to protecting the lives and property rights of citizens.[3] He enjoyed the support of newspaper magnate William Randolph Hearst as a presidential candidate in 1932, and won the California primary contest in May. Placed in nomination at the Democratic national convention in Chicago in June, Garner found himself locked in a stalemate with Franklin D. Roosevelt and two other rivals. Breaking the deadlock, Hearst prevailed upon Garner, who was in Washington, to release his delegates to Roosevelt. In doing so, Garner gained sufficient favor with FDR that he was selected as his running mate.[4] For many, Garner was viewed as a counterweight to the progressive, internationalist Roosevelt. He subsequently found himself in opposition of the Supreme Court, and some New Deal legislative initiatives. He was also among those in his party who opposed a third term for President Roosevelt.

Like his predecessors, Garner, as Vice President, maintained offices on Capitol Hill, but he did not regard himself as primarily a legislative officer. He regularly attended and actively participated in Cabinet meetings, often advised the President, and, particularly during the early years of the New Deal, often provided liaison to Congress. Although the Vice President was not among those formally designated to attend the deliberations of the emergency coordinating councils successively created by the President,[5] there is evidence that Garner was welcomed to, and did attend, a few meetings of the National

---

[3] Arthur M. Schlesinger, Jr., *The Crisis of the Old Order, 1919-1933* (Boston: Houghton Mifflin, 1957), p. 228.
[4] Ibid., pp. 307-309.
[5] These were the Executive Council, created by E.O. 6202-A of July 11, 1933; the National Emergency Council, established by E.O. 6433-A of Nov. 17, 1933; and the reconstituted National Emergency Council mandated by E.O. 6889-A of Oct. 29, 1934.

Emergency Council.[6] In 1935, after traveling with a congressional delegation – the first instance of a Vice President going abroad – for the installation of Manuel Quezon as the president of the Philippine Islands and to Japan to visit Emperor Hirohito, Garner undertook a foreign assignment for FDR, journeying to Mexico.[7]

HENRY A. WALLACE

Twenty years younger than Garner, Henry A. Wallace, trained in agricultural science, successor to his father as the editor of his family's magazine, and a former Republican, became an active supporter of FDR in 1932. He joined the Roosevelt Administration as Secretary of Agriculture in 1933, remaining in that position until September 1940, when he resigned to accept the Democratic nomination for Vice President. Serving the entirety of Roosevelt's third term, Wallace found his presidential ambitions stymied by FDR's decision to seek reelection in 1944. Furthermore, Wallace's liberal, internationalist views had produced strong opposition among party leaders to his re-nomination as Roosevelt's vice presidential running mate. Three months after his vice presidential term ended, he was nominated to be Secretary of Commerce, a position he held until September 1946, when President Harry S. Truman asked him to resign because of a speech attacking the administration's foreign policy toward the Soviet Union.

FDR selected Wallace to join him on the Democratic ticket in 1940 largely because he wanted a Vice President who was an internationalist, aware of world conditions, and especially alert to the menace of Nazism. War had begun in Europe in September 1939, but the United States remained officially neutral, even though American weaponry was being sold to Great Britain and France. Vice President Wallace could express critical views about the actions of Germany and Italy that the President, in view of official neutrality policy, could not. Shortly after the election, Roosevelt dispatched the Spanish-speaking Wallace to Mexico as his representative at the presidential

---

[6] These include meetings of Jan. 23, 1934; Jan. 8 and Feb. 5, 1935; and Jan. 28, 1936. See Lester G. Seligman and Elmer E. Cornwell, Jr., eds., *New Deal Mosaic: Roosevelt Confers with His National Emergency Council, 1933-1936* (Eugene, OR: University of Oregon Books, 1965), pp. 48, 68-69, 76, 400, 425, 426, 432-434, 437, 439-440, 502, 507, 516-517, 521.
[7] Irving G. Williams, *The Rise of the Vice Presidency* (Washington, DC: Public Affairs, 1956), pp. 161-162.

inauguration of Avila Camacho, a move designed to gain Mexican support for Pan-Americanism and hemispheric defense.[8] Later, in 1943, Wallace made a goodwill tour of Latin America.[9] The following year, he served as FDR's emissary to Soviet Siberia and China.[10]

When the President established the Economic Defense Board (later known as the Board of Economic Warfare) in July 1941, "for the purpose of developing and coordinating policies, plans, and programs designed to protect and strengthen the international economic relations of the United States in the interest of national defense," Wallace was made its chairman.[11] Shortly thereafter, he was made chairman of a related defense coordination entity, the Supply Priorities and Allocations Board.[12] In October 1941, Wallace joined Secretary of War Henry L. Stimson, Army Chief of Staff George C. Marshall, presidential science advisor Vannevar Bush, and Harvard University president James B. Conant as a member of the President's policy committee on the development and use of atomic energy.[13] A few weeks later, after the attack on Pearl Harbor, Wallace "alone attended both of the conferences President Roosevelt held that Sunday evening with the Cabinet and legislative leaders."[14]

HARRY S. TRUMAN

A farmer, World War I veteran, small businessman, and county judge in his home state of Missouri, Harry S. Truman was elected to the U.S. Senate in 1934 and served there until 1945 when he took the vice presidential oath. As a Senator, he came to be known as a man of personal integrity, a reputation that grew as a result of his chairmanship of the Senate Special Committee to Investigate the National Defense Program. The panel's various inquiries and remedial recommendations resulted in many economies and better equipment

---

[8] Ibid., pp. 182-183.
[9] Michael Dorman, *The Second Man* (New York: Delacorte, 1968), p. 155.
[10] Williams, *The Rise of the Vice Presidency*, pp. 202-204.
[11] See E.O. 8839, 3 C.F.R., 1938-1943 Comp., pp. 972-973; Dorman, *The Second Man*, pp. 152-155; Williams, *The Rise of the Vice Presidency*, pp. 186-188, 191-199.
[12] See E.O. 8875, 3 C.F.R., 1938-1943 Comp., pp. 993-995.
[13] Williams, *The Rise of the Vice Presidency*, p. 188.
[14] Ibid., p. 190.

and conditions for armed services personnel.[15] President Roosevelt selected Truman as his 1944 running mate after strong opposition developed among party leaders regarding the re-nomination of Vice President Henry A. Wallace. In an ironic twist, Truman helped secure Senate approval of his predecessor's appointment to be Secretary of Commerce in 1945. After serving only 82 days as Vice President, Truman suddenly found himself elevated to the presidency when FDR died on April 12, 1945. During his brief vice presidential tenure, Truman had been told very little by the very ill and very preoccupied President – American development of the atomic bomb being one of the more important non-admissions.[16]

ALBEN W. BARKLEY

Seven years older than President Truman, Alben Barkley practiced law in his native Kentucky, serving both as a county prosecutor and judge for a few years prior to being elected to the U.S. House of Representatives, where he served from 1913 through the early months of 1927. He successfully ran for the Senate in 1926, and remained in that institution until being sworn in as Vice President on January 20, 1949. During his Senate tenure, Barkley was the Democratic majority leader during 1937-1947 and minority leader in 1947-1948. After his vice presidential service, he was again elected to the Senate in 1954, serving there until his death in April 1956.

In the Senate, Barkley had admired Truman, instinctively, because he "voted right."[17] That admiration did not dim when FDR selected Truman as his running mate in 1944, a position Barkley himself sought. Actually, it was the President Roosevelt's maneuvering that angered Barkley, despite his selection to nominate FDR as the party's presidential candidate.[18] Four years later, Barkley arrived at the position he had sought. Although, by one

---

[15] See Donald H. Riddle, *The Truman Committee: A Study in Congressional Responsibility* (New Brunswick, NJ: Rutgers University Press, 1964).

[16] Truman's Senate committee investigators had come upon evidence of the so-called Manhattan Project for developing the atomic bomb, but when he confronted the Secretary of War with their findings, he was strongly advised to drop his inquiry, which he did. See Theodore Wilson, "The Truman Committee, " in Arthur M. Schlesinger, Jr., and Roger Bruns, eds., *Congress Investigates: A Documented History, 1792-1974*, vol. 4 (New York: Chelsea House, 1975), pp. 3134-3135.

[17] David McCullough, *Truman* (New York: Simon and Schuster, 1992), pp. 220, 226.

[18] Ibid., p. 313.

estimate, "his term of office saw little significant activity," he did "provide a useful link to Congress at times."[19] Barkley also regularly attended and participated in Cabinet deliberations; became the first Vice President to sit on the National Security Council,[20] which was "considered the most meaningful advance in the vice presidency until that time;"[21] and once flew to the front lines in Korea to eat Thanksgiving dinner with American troops.[22] Moreover, he "represented Truman at all sorts of political meetings, community events and other occasions throughout the United States and abroad."[23] Indeed, he thought well enough of Barkley that, despite some misgivings regarding the Vice President's age, Truman was prepared to endorse him as the party's presidential candidate in 1952.[24]

RICHARD M. NIXON

The man who did receive the Democratic presidential nomination in 1952 was Adlai E. Stevenson, Jr., not Alben Barkley. He was overwhelmed in the subsequent election by the very popular Dwight D. Eisenhower, who had Richard M. Nixon as his running mate. Trained as an attorney, Nixon had practiced law for a few years, worked briefly for the Office for Emergency Management in Washington, DC, and then entered naval service during World War II. Returning to civilian life in 1946, Nixon successfully ran for the House of Representatives, serving there from 1947 through 1950. Successfully elected to the Senate in November 1950, he took his seat early, the following month, with an appointment to fill a vacancy. He left the Senate on January 20, 1953, to begin serving as Vice President.

By one estimate, Nixon "exercised greater power and responsibility in the 1953-57 term than had any of his predecessors" as Vice President.[25] An active presidential liaison with Congress and presidential representative in

---

[19] Joel K. Goldstein, *The Modern American Vice President* (Princeton, NJ: Princeton University Press, 1982), p. 137.

[20] See 63 Stat. 578, adding the Vice President to the statutorily specified members of the National Security Council.

[21] Dorman, *The Second Man*, p. 193.

[22] Ibid., pp. 193-194; Williams, *The Rise of the Vice Presidency*, p. 233.

[23] Dorman, *The Second Man*, p. 194.

[24] Harry S. Truman, *Years of Trial and Hope* (Garden City, NY: Doubleday, 1956), p. 495.

[25] Williams, *The Rise of the Vice Presidency*, p. 235.

Republican political campaigns, he also served Eisenhower as a special envoy, undertaking seven such missions, during which he visited 54 countries.[26]

Nixon also filled some important institutional roles. He attended 163 Cabinet meetings, 19 of which, in accordance with President Eisenhower's instructions, he chaired; and of the 217 National Security Council sessions at which he was present, Nixon presided over 26 of these gatherings.[27] Other duties included chairing the Government Contract Committee, established by the President with E.O. 10479 of August 13, 1953; the panel was mandated to enforce anti-discrimination clauses in government contracts with private businesses.[28] Reporting in early 1955, the committee indicated it had secured compliance in 37 of 79 cases and continued it efforts during the years of Eisenhower's presidency until it was superseded by the President's Committee on Equal Employment Opportunity in 1961.[29] Early in 1959, when Eisenhower created the Cabinet Committee on Price Stability for Economic Growth to recommend policies to control inflation, he made Nixon the panel's chairman.[30]

LYNDON B. JOHNSON

Although Nixon sought to succeed President Eisenhower, he narrowly lost the 1960 election to John F. Kennedy, who had selected Lyndon B. Johnson as his running mate. LBJ had begun his public service career in 1932 as a secretary to a member of the U.S. House of Representatives, then became director of the National Youth Administration for Texas in 1935, prior to being selected in 1937 to fill a House vacancy. Reelected to the House five times, he saw active duty in the Navy during 1941-1942, and, after an unsuccessful campaign in 1941, was elected to the Senate in 1948. Becoming the Democratic leader in 1953, he was reelected to the Senate in 1954 and 1960, serving as the Senate majority leader from 1955 until he resigned in 1961 to become Vice President.

---

[26] Goldstein, *The Modern American Vice Presidency*, p. 159.

[27] Ibid., p. 168.

[28] 3 C.F.R. 1949-1953 Comp., pp. 961-962.

[29] Williams, *The Rise of the Vice Presidency*, p. 248; 3 C.F.R.

[30] U.S. General Services Administration, National Archives and Records Service, *Public Papers of the Presidents of the United States: Dwight D. Eisenhower, 1959* (Washington: GPO, 1961), p. 485.

Johnson regularly attended Cabinet and National Security Council meetings, but apparently did not chair sessions of the former, and President Kennedy convened an executive committee of National Security Council members and other officials rather than holding formal council deliberations. (LBJ was also a member of the committee). In addition, Johnson served the President as an adviser and a liaison to Congress. As a special envoy, he made 10 trips during which he visited a total of 23 countries.[31]

While giving Johnson various institutional roles, Kennedy also assigned his Vice President office space in the Executive Office Building next to the White House.[32] For the first time, the Vice President had an executive office in addition to, and apart from, his Senate facilities on Capitol Hill.[33] Creating the President's Committee on Equal Employment Opportunity, the 1961 successor to Eisenhower's Government Contract Committee, Kennedy made Johnson its chairman.[34] The President also named Johnson to head the National Aeronautics and Space Council,[35] an entity within the Executive Office of the President,[36] and to lead the Peace Corps National Advisory Council.[37]

HUBERT H. HUMPHREY

The November 1963 assassination of President Kennedy elevated Johnson to the presidency, and the nation was without a Vice President until 1965, when LBJ, elected in a landslide, was joined by Hubert H. Humphrey. A former mayor of Minneapolis, Humphrey was initially elected to the Senate in 1948, and was returned in each of his successive election campaigns. Johnson reportedly was eager to have his assistance, and, by one estimate, no previous

---

[31] Goldstein, *The Modern American Vice President*, p. 159.

[32] This development launched the institutionalization of the Vice President's executive office, which is reviewed in Appendix 2 of this report.

[33] Paul C. Light, *Vice-Presidential Power* (Baltimore, MD: John Hopkins University Press, 1984), p. 68.

[34] See E.O. 10925, 3 C.F.R., 1959-1963 Comp., pp. 448-454.

[35] U.S. General Services Administration, National Archives and Records Service, *Public Papers of the President of the United States: John F. Kennedy, 1961* (Washington: GPO, 1962), p. 309.

[36] As originally chartered in 1958 (72 Stat. 427), the council was chaired by the President, but, at Kennedy's request, Congress assigned the panel's leadership position to the Vice President in 1961 (75 Stat. 46).

[37] Dorman, *The Second Man*, pp. 254-255.

Vice President "was used by his President in such a broad variety of roles."[38] However, it has also been observed that "Johnson showed little interest in his own Vice President," and Humphrey's willingness to assume so many roles was not merely a result of his energy and enthusiasm, but was more antidote to his "increasing isolation from policy" – an estrangement attributable, in large measure, to Humphrey's desires to deescalate U.S. military involvement in Vietnam and to negotiate a settlement of the hostilities in that region.[39]

Like his immediate predecessors, Humphrey attended Cabinet meetings and National Security Council sessions, but probably did not perform the same liaison to Congress as Johnson had for Kennedy. As a special envoy, he took 12 trips to a total of 31 countries.[40] He chaired the National Aeronautics and Space Council and the Peace Corps National Advisory Council, but the President's Equal Employment Opportunity Commission was abolished, and its responsibilities were assigned to the Civil Service Commission and the Department of Labor.[41] Humphrey headed a related, short-lived coordination and policy-recommending panel, the President's Council on Equal Opportunity,[42] and Congress created another statutory leadership role for him by assigning the Vice President the chairmanship of the new National Council on Marine Resources and Engineering Development.[43] In the spring of 1967, LBJ began assigning the Vice President responsibility for chairing various presidential policy-planning and coordinating panels, including the President's Council on Youth Opportunity,[44] the President's Council on Physical Fitness and Sports,[45] the National Council on Indian Opportunity,[46] and the President's Council on Recreation and Natural Beauty.[47]

---

[38] Ibid., p. 274.

[39] Light, *Vice-Presidential Power*, p. 32; also see Hubert H. Humphrey, *The Education of a Public Man* (Garden City, NY: Doubleday, 1976), pp. 314-353, 355-359.

[40] Goldstein, *The Modern American Vice Presidency*, p. 159.

[41] See E.O. 11246, 3 C.F.R., 1964-1965 Comp., pp. 339-348; Goldstein, *The Modern American Vice Presidency*, p. 155.

[42] See E.O. 11197, 3 C.F.R. 1964-1965 Comp., pp. 278-280.

[43] See 80 Stat. 204.

[44] See E.O. 11330, 3 C.F.R., 1966-1970 Comp., pp. 622-624.

[45] See E.O. 11398, 3 C.F.R., 1966-1970 Comp., pp. 714-716.

[46] See E.O. 11399, 3 C.F.R., 1966-1970 Comp., pp. 717.

[47] See E.O. 11402, 3 C.F.R., 1966-1970 Comp., p. 719.

SPIRO T. AGNEW

When Johnson declined to seek his party's presidential nomination in 1968, Humphrey became the standard-bearer, but was defeated by Richard M. Nixon, whose running mate, Spiro T. Agnew, became Vice President. An attorney and county government official, Agnew had been elected governor of Maryland in 1966. As Vice President, he began presiding over the deliberations of the Senate with no prior legislative experience, and he apparently devoted little of his time to this responsibility.[48] Agnew was also ill-prepared for congressional liaison duties on behalf of the President, but he did undertake special envoy assignments, making seven trips to a total of 28 countries.[49]

Agnew met with the Cabinet and the National Security Council, but other leadership roles were eliminated or never offered. The National Council on Marine Resources and Engineering Development became dormant and was eventually terminated in June 1971.[50] Nixon eliminated the President's Council on Recreation and Natural Beauty,[51] and reconstituted the President's Council on Physical Fitness and Sports with the President's consultant on physical fitness as the chair.[52] Other such panels apparently did not interest the Vice President. According to one account, "Agnew was not an activist Vice-President and did not want many assignments," two exceptions being the National Aeronautics and Space Council, which was subsequently abolished by presidential reorganization plan in 1973,[53] and the new Office of Intergovernmental Relations, but he "had trouble with both."[54] Established less than a month after the inauguration as an Executive Office agency, the Office of Intergovernmental Relations was placed under the immediate supervision of the Vice President and was created to make use of Agnew's experience in state and local government matters.[55] Nixon's displeasure with the Vice President's performance prompted him to remove Agnew from

---

[48] Goldstein, *The Modern American Vice Presidency*, p. 142; Light, *Vice-Presidential Power*, p. 43.
[49] Goldstein, *The Modern American Vice Presidency*, p. 159; see also pp. 160, 166.
[50] See 84 Stat. 865.
[51] See E.O. 11472, 3 C.F.R., 1966-1970 Comp., pp. 792-795.
[52] See E.O. 11562, 3 C.F.R. 1966-1970 Comp., pp. 970-972.
[53] See 87 Stat. 1089.
[54] Light, *Vice-Presidential Power*, p. 33.
[55] See E.O. 11455, 3 C.F.R., 1966-1970 Comp., pp. 775-777.

intergovernmental affairs following the 1972 elections, and the Office of Intergovernmental Relations was abolished.[56]

The Vice President was made a member, but not the chair or the head, of some other presidential entities, such as the Council for Urban Affairs,[57] the Cabinet Committee on Economic Policy,[58] the Environmental Quality Council,[59] the Council for Rural Affairs,[60] and the Domestic Council.[61]

There is evidence that the President and some of his senior assistants became sufficiently disappointed with Agnew's performance during Nixon's first term that he was almost replaced by former Texas governor John B. Connally as the Republican vice presidential nominee for the 1972 campaign.[62] Agnew, however, was retained by Nixon and was reelected with him. Then, seven months after the inauguration, Agnew received notice that he was under investigation by the U.S. attorney for Maryland concerning alleged kickbacks from private architectural and engineering firms that had been improperly awarded state and federal contracts during Agnew's county executive, gubernatorial, and vice presidential years. The investigation continued, and, after other efforts to contend with the multiple charges against him failed, Agnew agreed to resign and avoid imprisonment by pleading no contest to a single charge of federal income tax evasion. His resignation occurred on October 10, 1973.

GERALD R. FORD

Under the terms of the 25th Amendment, Gerald R. Ford, a member of the House of Representatives since 1949 and House minority leader since 1965, was nominated by President Nixon on October 12, 1973, to succeed Agnew as Vice President. Ford was subsequently confirmed by the Senate on November 27 and by the House on December 6. He resigned from the House the same

---

[56] See Light, *Vice-Presidential Power*, p. 33; E.O. 11690 3 C.F.R., 1971-1975 Comp., pp. 732-734.

[57] See E.O. 11452, 3 C.F.R. 1966-1970 Comp., pp. 772-773.

[58] See E.O. 11453, 3 C.F.R. 1966-1970 Comp., pp. 773-774.

[59] See E.O. 11472, 3 C.F.R. 1966-1970 Comp., pp. 792-795.

[60] See E.O. 11493, 3 C.F.R. 1966-1970 Comp., pp. 876-877.

[61] See 84 Stat. 2085.

[62] See Goldstein, *The Modern American Vice Presidency*, p. 171; Light, *Vice-Presidential Power*, pp. 33, 46, 107.

day his colleagues approved his nomination, and was sworn in as Vice President.

As Ford began his new duties, revelations about the so-called Watergate incident – the June 17, 1972, burglary at the Democratic National Committee headquarters located in the Watergate office building in Washington, DC – had already captured public attention. Five men had been arrested and were subsequently brought to trial in January 1973. Revelations about the larger implications of the break-in had been appearing in the *Washington Post*, which, in early October 1972, had charged that "the Watergate bugging incident stemmed from a massive campaign of political spying and sabotage conducted on behalf of President Nixon's reelection."[63] Subsequently, investigations by a Senate Select Committee on Presidential Campaign Activities, the House Committee on the Judiciary, and federal prosecutors revealed the truth of this allegation.

Ford warily observed these unfolding disclosures as he moved from the House to the vice presidency. Remaining largely "aloof from the executive branch" as Vice President,[64] he did chair the newly established Domestic Council Committee on the Right of Privacy,[65] which, among other pursuits, assisted with the development of the Privacy Act of 1974.[66] As the investigations of the Watergate incident and related matters continued, Ford, "spent little time in Washington as Vice President and rarely interceded with Congress" on behalf of the President.[67]

On May 9, 1974, in closed session, members of the House Committee on the Judiciary began considering the evidence concerning the President's possible involvement in the Watergate break-in and cover-up. At the end of the month, the Supreme Court agreed to hear arguments on President Nixon's claim of executive privilege to withhold evidence subpoenaed by Special Prosecutor Leon Jaworski for use in a Watergate-related trial. On the morning of July 24, a unanimous Court upheld Jaworski's subpoena to President

---

[63] Carl Bernstein and Bob Woodward, "FBI Finds Nixon Aides Sabotaged Democrats," *Washington Post*, Oct. 10, 1972, pp. A1, A 14.

[64] Goldstein, *The Modern American Vice Presidency*, p. 156.

[65] The committee was established by presidential announcement on Feb. 23, 1974; see Office of the White House Press Secretary, "Fact Sheet: The President's Address on the American Right of Privacy," Washington, DC, Feb. 23, 1974 (copy in author's possession).

[66] Ironically, by the time Congress cleared the Privacy Act for presidential approval, Ford had succeeded to the presidency and he signed the measure; see 88 Stat. 1896.

[67] Goldstein, *The Modern American Vice Presidency*, p. 180.

Nixon.[68] That evening, the Committee on the Judiciary, in open session, began its discussion of the impeachment of the President. Six days later, the panel approved three articles of impeachment, recommending to the House that the President be impeached and removed from office for violating his constitutional oath by obstruction of justice in the Watergate cover-up, by abuse of his presidential powers in various ways, and by contempt of Congress in refusing to comply with the committee's subpoena.[69]

Conceding that the disclosure "may further damage my case," Nixon, on August 8, released the transcripts of three conversations that he had held with White House chief of staff H.R. Haldeman on June 23, 1972, shortly after the Watergate burglary.[70] Congressional support for the President almost disappeared with the revelation of these conversations. After meeting with congressional leaders on August 7 and 8, 1974, Nixon announced in a broadcast address to the nation on the evening of the second day that he was resigning from office, saying, "it has become evident to me that I no longer have a strong enough political base in the Congress to justify continuing [the] effort" to withstand impeachment and stay in office.[71] The following day, his letter of resignation reached the Secretary of State shortly after 11:30 a.m. and was accepted.[72] Vice President Ford succeeded to the presidency.

NELSON A. ROCKEFELLER

Pursuant to the terms of the 25th Amendment, President Ford nominated Nelson A. Rockefeller to be Vice President on August 20, 1974. The Senate confirmed the selection on December 10, and the House followed, giving its approval on December 19 and clearing the way for the administration of the oath of office in the Senate chamber that same day. Rockefeller had begun government service in 1940 as the head of the Office for Coordination of Commercial and Cultural Relations between the American Republics, which

---

[68] *United States v. Nixon*, 418 U.S. 683 (1974).

[69] See U.S. Congress, House Committee on the Judiciary, *Impeachment of Richard M. Nixon, President of the United States*, 93rd Cong., 2nd sess., H.Rept. 93-1305 (Washington: GPO, 1974).

[70] U.S. General Services Administration, National Archives and Records Service, *Public Papers of the Presidents of the United States, Richard Nixon, 1974* (Washington: GPO, 1975), pp. 621-623.

[71] Ibid., pp. 626-629.

[72] Ibid., p. 633.

later became the Office of the Coordinator of Inter-American Affairs in 1941. He left the leadership of this latter entity in 1944 to become assistant secretary of state for American republics affairs, serving until August 1945. Rockefeller returned to the federal government in 1950, serving as the chairman of President Truman's International Development Advisory Board, which reviewed the U.S. "Point Four" program for technical assistance abroad. Subsequently, in 1953, President Eisenhower appointed him chairman of the President's Advisory Committee on Governmental Organization, a position he held until 1958. In addition, Rockefeller was made undersecretary of health, education, and welfare in 1953, then moved to the White House in 1954 to be a special assistant to President Eisenhower. He was initially elected governor of New York in 1959 and, with successive reelections, served through 1973. Rockefeller also was President Nixon's personal representative to Latin America in 1969, and he served on the President's Foreign Intelligence Advisory Board during 1969-1974.

Rockefeller came to the vice presidency eager to assist the President, and the formulation of domestic policy was a major area of interest to him. He began as "an active participant" in the Ford Administration, but quickly "was frozen out of the policy process" for several reasons, most of which concerned his assumption of institutional roles.[73] Shortly after his confirmation as Vice President, Rockefeller sought to be the de facto head of the Domestic Council and, thereby, serve as the primary conduit of domestic policy proposals to the President. Ford initially agreed to this agreement, then had second thoughts after conferring with some senior White House assistants, but was finally swayed by Rockefeller. The incident, however, won Rockefeller the enmity of some important White House aides, including chief of staff Donald Rumsfeld.[74] Moreover, Rockefeller was not an active or effective promoter of administration policies with Congress.[75]

Rockefeller also accepted assignments involving significant commitments of time, energy, and political capital, which not only subjected him to bureaucratic conflicts, but also further involved him in policy disputes with White House assistants and senior administration officials. Primary among

---

[73] See Light, *Vice-Presidential Power*, p. 180.
[74] See Goldstein, *The Modern American Vice Presidency*, pp. 171-172; Robert T. Hartmann, *Palace Politics* (New York: McGraw-Hill, 1980), pp. 304-311, 354-359; Light, *Vice-Presidential Power*, pp. 183-184, 187-192.
[75] Goldstein, *The Modern American Vice Presidency*, p. 180.

these was his leadership of the Domestic Council and his chairmanship of the Commission on CIA Activities within the United States.[76] In addition, Rockefeller headed such panels as the National Commission on Productivity and Work Quality,[77] the President's Panel on Federal Compensation,[78] and the National Study Commission on Water Quality.[79] He was a member, as well, of the Commission on the Organization of the Government for the Conduct of Foreign Policy.[80]

WALTER F. MONDALE

Although Rockefeller was not Ford's running mate in the 1976 election campaign, the contest was won by the opposition, bringing Jimmy Carter to the presidency and Walter F. Mondale to the vice presidency. A practicing attorney and former Minnesota attorney general, Mondale had been appointed to fill the Senate seat of Hubert H. Humphrey, who had resigned in 1964 preparatory to becoming Vice President. Mondale had remained in the Senate, being elected in 1966 and returned in 1972.

At Carter's insistence, Mondale was given an office in the West Wing of the White House, in close proximity to the Oval Office.[81] (Agnew was the first Vice President to occupy space there, but, isolated from his own staff and pressured by the White House chief of staff, moved out after a brief stay.) Furthermore, immediately after the election, the two men had agreed that Mondale would not be burdened with various secondary roles, but, in the President's words, "would truly be second in command, involved in every aspect of governing."[82] The vitiation of the vice presidency as a legislative position was now, if not before, complete: executive duties were the priority

---

[76] For the commission's mandate, see E.O. 11828, 3 C.F.R., 1971-1975 Comp., pp. 933-934; also see Light, *Vice-Presidential Power*, pp. 184-187.

[77] See 85 Stat. 753; 88 Stat. 236.

[78] See U.S. General Services Administration, National Archives and Records Service, *Public Papers of the Presidents of the United States: Gerald R. Ford, 1975* (Washington: GPO, 1977), p. 813.

[79] See 86 Stat. 875.

[80] See 86 Stat. 497.

[81] Jimmy Carter, *Keeping Faith* (New York: Bantam, 1982), p. 40; Light, *Vice-Presidential Power*, pp. 76-77.

[82] Carter, *Keeping Faith*, p. 39; also see Goldstein, *The Modern American Vice Presidency*, p. 157; Light, *Vice-Presidential Power*, pp. 47-48, 206-208.

of the office. Indeed, during his first year as Vice President, Mondale devoted a total of only 18 hours to presiding over the Senate.[83]

Mondale made 14 trips to a total of 35 countries, often functioning as a presidential policy agent.[84] He functioned as the President's "general adviser," being, in Carter's view, "the only person that I have, with both the substantive knowledge and political stature to whom I can turn over a major assignment."[85] Furthermore, the Vice President's role was enhanced by the respect accorded him and his staff by the President's senior assistants, by the "impressive and dignified assignments" given to him by the President amid "conditions under which Mondale could be an effective counselor," by complete information sharing, and by structured meetings with the President as well as the right to participate in any conference unless asked to leave.[86] He also proved valuable concerning White House relations with Congress – initially, in acquainting senior presidential aides with congressional structure, operations, and culture, and also in providing some Members of Congress a trustworthy conduit to the President.[87]

GEORGE H. W. BUSH

The unsuccessful reelection effort of Carter and Mondale in 1980 brought Ronald Reagan to the presidency, with George H. W. Bush as his Vice President. An experienced public servant, Bush had been a two-term member of the House of Representatives; ambassador to the United Nations and Republican National Committee chairman during the Nixon Administration; U.S. diplomatic representative to the People's Republic of China and Director of Central Intelligence during the Ford Administration; and a candidate for the Republican presidential nomination in 1980.

Reagan scarcely knew Bush before agreeing to his selection, almost as an afterthought, as an acceptable running mate who would never become a

---

[83] Goldstein, *The Modern American Vice Presidency*, p. 142.
[84] See Ibid., pp. 159, 161-162, 166.
[85] See Ibid., pp. 172-173; also see Light, *Vice-Presidential Power*, pp. 201-202.
[86] Goldstein, *The Modern American Vice Presidency*, pp. 150, 173-174, 221; Light, *Vice-Presidential Power*, pp. 208-212, 218-220.
[87] Goldstein, *The Modern American Vice Presidency*, pp. 180-181.

confidant to the President.[88] However, even though the two men were not very well acquainted with each other, Bush was "intensely loyal" to Reagan and remained in his shadow.[89] For his part, Reagan "came to enjoy Bush's company around the office," but the two men and their wives did not socialize.[90]

Bush retained Mondale's West Wing office, had at least weekly private meetings with the President, and enjoyed the added benefit of having his old friend and 1980 campaign manager, James Baker III, serving as White House chief of staff. He was also more willing than Mondale had been to take on various secondary roles.[91] Bush was made a member of each of the five initial Cabinet councils formed at the outset of the Reagan Administration,[92] and also served on the subsequently created Economic Policy Council and Domestic Policy Council.[93] He also was made the chairman of the Presidential Task Force on Regulatory Relief,[94] the National Security Council's crisis management team,[95] the South Florida Task Force on Drug Abuse and Trafficking Prevention,[96] an interagency action group in mitigating economic

---

[88] Bob Schieffer and Gary Paul Gates, *The Acting President* (New York: E.P. Dutton, 1989), p. 313.

[89] Ibid., p. 318.

[90] Ibid.; also see Light, *Vice-Presidential Power*, p. 266.

[91] Light, *Vice-Presidential Power*, pp.260-261, 264.

[92] See U.S. General Services Administration, National Archives and Records Service, *Public Papers of the Presidents of the United States: Ronald Reagan, 1981* (Washington: GPO, 1982), pp. 166-167; on the work of the Cabinet councils, see Chester A. Newland, "Executive Office Policy Apparatus: Enforcing the Reagan Agenda," in Lester M. Salamon and Michael S. Lund, eds., *The Reagan Presidency and the Governing of America* (Washington: Urban Institute, 1985), pp. 153-161; James P. Pfiffner, *The Strategic Presidency* (Chicago, IL: Dorsey, 1988), pp. 58-67.

[93] See U.S. General Services Administration, National Archives and Records Service, *Public Papers of the Presidents of the United States: Ronald Reagan, 1985* (Washington: GPO, 1988), p. 419.

[94] See U.S. General Services Administration, National Archives and Records Service, *Public Papers of the Presidents of the United States: Ronald Reagan, 1981*, pp. 30-31; Light, *Vice-Presidential Power*, p. 261.

[95] See U.S. General Services Administration, National Archives and Records Service, *Public Papers of the Presidents of the United States: Ronald Reagan, 1981*, p. 285; Light, *Vice-Presidential Power*, pp. 261-262.

[96] See U.S. General Services Administration, National Archives and Records Service, *Public Papers of the Presidents of the United States: Ronald Reagan, 1982* (Washington: GPO, 1983), pp. 1252, 1314, 1488-1491.

hardship in the southwest border region,[97] and the Vice President's Task Force on Combating Terrorism.[98]

Bush apparently retained the influential presidential advisory role established by Mondale, but it was by no means a guaranteed status for future successors. Such influence, it has been observed, "remains conditioned by factors that evolve with each new administration."[99]

DANFORTH QUAYLE

Elected to the presidency in 1988, Bush was joined by Dan Quayle as Vice President. After working briefly as a journalist and Indiana state government official, Quayle was elected in 1976 to the House of Representatives, where he served until being elected to the Senate in 1980. Returned to the Senate in 1986, he was Bush's surprise choice as his running mate in 1988. The two men apparently had come to know each other when the young Senator began to stop by Bush's Capitol Hill office to chat, but they were not particularly close or well acquainted.[100] On the eve of the opening of the Republican national convention, when Bush met with several major senior campaign advisers to discuss the vice presidential candidate, Quayle was one of seven top choices to be named as a possible running mate – "the one most often proposed by his knowledgeable circle of political pros."[101] His subsequent selection stunned many, and some considered it an impulsive decision by Bush.[102] When he invited him to join the ticket, Bush reportedly told Quayle that he was "the first choice, and my only choice."[103] After the election, Bush offered some plausible reasons for his decision, but the strong

---

[97] See U.S. General Services Administration, National Archives and Records Service, *Public Papers of the Presidents of the United States: Ronald Reagan, 1983* (Washington: GPO, 1985), p. 1160.

[98] See U.S. General Services Administration, National Archives and Records Service, *Public Papers of the Presidents of the United States: Ronald Reagan, 1985*, p. 800.

[99] Light, *Vice-Presidential Power*, p. 268.

[100] Jack W. Germond and Jules Witcover, *Whose Broad Stripes and Bright Stars?* (New York: Warner, 1989), p. 374.

[101] Ibid., p. 379.

[102] Burt A. Rockman, "The Leadership Style of George Bush," in Colin Campbell and Bert A. Rockman, eds., *The Bush Presidency: First Appraisals* (Chatham, NJ: Chatham House, 1991), p. 30.

[103] Germond and Witcover, *Whose Broad Stripes and Bright Stars?*, p. 385.

likelihood of Quayle's giving unswerving loyalty to the President probably was a crucially persuasive factor.[104]

Quayle retained a West Wing office, "only a few feet away from the Oval Office," and had a routine weekly luncheon meeting with the President.[105] He also regularly attended Cabinet and National Security Council meetings. Quayle's other institutional roles included chairing a task force that came to be known as the Council on Competitiveness.[106] An extension of the Presidential Task Force on Regulatory Relief, which Bush had led during his vice presidency tenure, the new panel soon became immersed in controversy concerning its alleged secrecy, interference in various aspects of regulatory policy and practice, and transgressions of ethics standards.[107] Quayle also was active as the chairman of the National Space Council,[108] which provided advice and assistance to the President on national space policy and strategy.[109]

As Bush committed American armed forces to combat in the Persian Gulf region in early 1991, Quayle's meetings with the President became more frequent, but his influence as an adviser in this area was not immediately

---

[104] See Ibid., p. 387.

[105] Dan Quayle, *Standing Firm* (New York: HarperCollins, 1994), pp. 86, 103-107.

[106] See U.S. National Archives and Records Administration, *Public Papers of the Presidents of the United States: George Bush, 1989* (Washington: GPO, 1990), pp. 76, 86; U.S. National Archives and Records Administration, *Public Papers of the Presidents of the United States: George Bush, 1990* (Washington, 1991), pp. 333, 833, 1094-1095.

[107] In chronological order, see, for example, Christine Triano, "Quayle and Co.," *Government Information Insider*, vol. 1, June 1991, pp. 6-8; Ann Devroy and David S. Broder, "Quayle Pressured Agencies to Ease Rules on Business, Groups Say," *Washington Post*, Sept. 8, 1991, p. A6; David S. Broder and Stan Hinden, "Quayle Requests Look at Breeden Testimony," *Washington Post*, Oct. 2, 1991, pp. C1, C3; "Still Meddling After All Theses Months," *The OMB Watcher*, vol. 9, Oct. 30, 1991; pp. 8-11; Dana Priest, "Competitiveness Council Suspected of Unduly Influencing Regulators," *Washington Post*, Nov. 18, 1991, p. A19; Michael Weisskopf, "Regulatory Adviser Has Stake in Chemical Firm," *Washington Post*, Nov. 20, 1991, p. A21; Dana Priest, "Competitiveness Council Under Scrutiny," *Washington Post*, Nov. 26, 1991, p. A 19; Michael Weisskopf, "Quayle Council Official Had Role in Acid Rain Rule Action," *Washington Post*, Dec. 6, 1991, p. A19; "Conflict on the Quayle Council," *The OMB Watcher*, vol. 9, Dec. 24, 1991, pp. 7-9; Christine Triano, "Dan's World," *Government Information Insider*, vol. 2, March 1991, pp. 2-3; "The Council on Competitiveness: Executive Oversight of Agency Rulemaking," *Administrative Law Journal of the American University*, vol. 7, Summer 1993, pp. 297-343; Charles Tiefer, *The Semi-Sovereign Presidency* (Boulder, CO: Westview, 1994), pp. 61-88.

[108] See 102 Stat. 4102.

[109] See U.S. National Archives and Records Administration, *Public Papers of the Presidents of the United States: George Bush, 1989*, pp. 456-457; David C. Morrison, "Vice President for Space," *National Journal*, vol. 21, July 29, 1989, pp. 1910-1915.

clear.[110] During the prosecution of the Gulf War, Bush, by one assessment, "seemed increasingly mature and self-assured," while Quayle "seemed to some as commensurately less so."[111] Bush retained Quayle as his running mate in 1992, but their reelection effort proved unsuccessful.

ALBERT GORE, JR.

The 1992 elections brought William J. Clinton to the presidency, and with him, Albert Gore, Jr., as Vice President. The son of a U.S. Senator, Gore arrived at the vice presidency after having served four terms in the House of Representatives and one term in the Senate. After mounting an unsuccessful bid to obtain the Democratic presidential nomination in 1988, Gore had been reelected to the Senate in 1990. He continued as Vice President during President Clinton's second term in office.

Beyond his participation in Cabinet and National Security Council meetings, Gore quickly became and remained one of the President's "most influential advisers."[112] One of the first special duties Clinton assigned his Vice President began shortly after the inauguration. On March 3, 1993, the President indicated he was initiating the National Performance Review (NPR) to be conducted by a task force headed by Gore. The goal, said Clinton, "is to make the entire Federal Government both less expensive and more efficient, and to change the culture of our national bureaucracy away from complacency and entitlement toward initiative and empowerment. We intend to redesign, to reinvent, to reinvigorate the entire National Government."[113] Gore led the NPR – which went through various phases and resulted in a multiplicity of assessments, initiatives, and reforms – to the final days of the Clinton Administration.[114]

---

[110] See Paul G. Kengor, "The Role of the Vice President During the Crisis in the Persian Gulf," *Presidential Studies Quarterly*, vol. 24, Fall 1994, pp. 783-807.

[111] Burt Solomon, "War Bolsters Quayle's Visibility...But Hasn't Increased His Stature," *National Journal*, vol. 23, Mar. 2, 1991, pp. 522-523.

[112] Elizabeth Drew, *Showdown* (New York: Simon and Schuster, 1996), p. 224.

[113] U.S. National Archives and Records Administration, *Public Papers of the Presidents of the United States: William J. Clinton, 1993* (Washington: GPO, 1994), pp. 233-235, 1944-1948.

[114] See U.S. Library of Congress, Congressional Research Service, *The National Performance Review and Other Government Reform Initiatives: An Overview, 1993-1999*, by Harold C. Relyea, Maricele J. Cornejo, Riemann, and Henry B. Hogue, CRS Report RL30596 (Washington: June 14, 2000).

During June and July, the Vice President, at the President's direction, worked with the relevant departments and agencies to identify problems and recommend solutions regarding border management and immigration policy.[115] Later, Gore represented the administration in a highly publicized November 1993 broadcast debate with former independent presidential candidate H. Ross Perot, supporting congressional approval of the North American Free Trade Agreement.[116] He also was designated by Clinton to lead a U.S. Russian Joint Commission on Energy and Space[117] and to chair the President's Community Enterprise Board, which was created to provide advice and coordination regarding various federal programs available to distressed communities.[118]

In the early years of his vice presidency, Gore, in the words of the President, "led the charge to make this administration a leader in the global environmental effort," and he continued to exert such leadership during his tenure.[119] At Clinton's direction, Gore established a working group on Indian economic development in 1994, in conjunction with the administration's community enterprise initiatives.[120] During the year, the President also named Gore to lead a U.S.-Russian Joint Commission on Economic and Technological Cooperation[121] and the Ounce of Prevention Council, which was charged with overseeing and coordinating the various crime prevention programs governed by the Violent Crime Control and Law Enforcement Act of 1994.[122]

The Vice President also assumed a major role regarding telecommunications and electronic information infrastructure policy and development,[123] aviation safety and security matters,[124] and electronic

---

[115] See U.S. National Archives and Records Administration, *Public Papers of the Presidents of the United States: William J. Clinton, 1993*, pp. 1194-1196.

[116] Ibid., pp. 1905, 1940-1941, 1944-1945.

[117] Ibid., pp. 1429, 1448.

[118] Ibid., pp. 1460-1462.

[119] U.S. National Archives and Records Administration, *Public Papers of the Presidents of the United States: William J. Clinton, 1994* (Washington: GPO, 1995), p. 742.

[120] Ibid., p. 802.

[121] Ibid., pp. 1643, 1652, 1660.

[122] Ibid., pp. 1542-2543.

[123] See, for example, U.S. National Archives and Records Administration, *Public Papers of the Presidents of the United States: William J. Clinton, 1996* (Washington: GPO, 1997), pp. 186-187, 191, 243, 257, 261, 344, 346, 404, 1802.

[124] Ibid., pp. 1201, 1219, 1259, 1289, 1416, 1506, 1650, 1728, 1750, 1794, 1796, 2193.

commerce strategy.[125] Gore's eight-year record of performance as Vice President awaits thorough scholarly analysis. The popular assessment of the man who sought to succeed President Clinton was seemingly favorable, though close, in the 2000 election, but he lost the electoral vote contest.

RICHARD B. CHENEY

Selected by Texas Governor George W. Bush to be his running mate, Richard B. Cheney comes to the vice presidency with a varied public service background. Gaining staff experience in a gubernatorial and congressional office before becoming a special assistant to the director of the Office of Economic Opportunity during 1969-1970, Cheney subsequently served as a White House staff assistance in 1971, assistant to director of the Cost of Living Council during 1971-1973, deputy assistant to the President during 1973-1975, and White House chief of staff during 1975-1976. Elected to the House of Representatives in 1978, he served there until 1989, when he was appointed Secretary of Defense during the Bush Administration. Returning to private life in 1992, Cheney became an oil industry, construction, and insurance company executive.

Having ruled out seeking the presidency himself, Cheney reportedly has begun his tenure with an integration of his vice presidential staff with that of the President, allowing the White House to speak and act with leadership unity as it deals with Congress and the public.[126]

Early assignments for Cheney include chairing a study commission on the developing national energy crisis and serving as a liaison to Congress. For this latter role, the Vice President has set up offices in the House as well as the Senate. The President has also asked him to be a principal spokesman for the administration, making himself especially available to the broadcast media. Bush is giving consideration to having Cheney chair the meetings of deputies from the Departments of State and Defense and the National Security Council.

---

[125] See, for example, U.S. National Archives and Records Administration, *Public Papers of the Presidents of the United States: William J. Clinton, 1998* (Washington: GPO, 2000), pp. 2095, 2101.
[126] Dana Milbank, "For Number Two, the Future Is Now," *Washington Post*, Feb. 3, 2001, p. A1.

The role, heretofore never held by a Vice President, would give Cheney an opportunity to recommend and influence foreign policy.[127]

APPENDIX 1: PRESIDENTS AND VICE PRESIDENTS OF THE UNITED STATES (WITH YEARS OF SERVICE)

George Washington (1789-1797)
    John Adams (1789-1797)
John Adams (1797-1801)
    Thomas Jefferson (1797-1801)
Thomas Jefferson (1801-1809)
    Aaron Burr (1801-1805)
    George Clinton (1805-1809)
James Madison (1809-1817)
    George Clinton (1809-1817)
    Elbridge Gerry (1813-1814)
James Monroe
    Daniel D. Tompkins (1817-1825)
John Quincy Adams (1825-1829)
    John C. Calhoun (1825-1829)
Andrew Jackson (1829-1837)
    John C. Calhoun (1829-1832)
    Martin Van Buren (1833-1837)
Martin Van Buren (1837-1841)
    Richard M. Johnson (1837-1841)
William Henry Harrison (1841)
    John Tyler (1841)
John Tyler (1841-1845)*
    vacant (1841-1845)
James K. Polk (1845-1849)
    George M. Dallas (1845-1849)
Zachary Taylor (1849-1850)
    Millard Fillmore (1849-1850)
Millard Fillmore (1850-1853)*
    vacant (1850-1853)

---

[127] Ibid., p. A14.

Franklin Pierce (1853-1857)
   William R. King (1853-1857)
James Buchanan (1857-1861)
   John C. Breckenridge (1857-1861)
Abraham Lincoln (1861-1865)
   Hannibal Hamlin (1861-1865)
   Andrew Johnson (1865)
Andrew Johnson (1865-1869)*
   vacant
Ulysses S. Grant (1869-1877)
   Schuyler Colfax (1869-1873)
   Henry Wilson (1873-1875)
Rutherford B. Hayes (1877-1881)
   William B. Wheeler (1877-1881)
James A. Garfield (1881)
   Chester A. Arthur (1881)
Chester A. Arthur (1881-1885)*
   vacant (1881-1885)
Grover Cleveland (1885-1889; 1893-1897)
   Thomas A. Hendricks (1885-1889)
   Adlai E. Stevenson (1893-1897)
Benjamin Harrison (1889-1893)
   Levi P. Morton (1889-1893)
William McKinley (1897-1901)
   Garret A. Hobart (1897-1901)
   Theodore Roosevelt (1901)
Theodore Roosevelt (1901-1909)*
   vacant (1901-1905)
   Charles W. Fairbanks (1905-1909)
William H. Taft (1909-1913)
   James S. Sherman (1909-1913)
Woodrow Wilson (1913-1921)
   Thomas R. Marshall (1913-1921)
Warren G. Harding (1921-1923)
   Calvin Coolidge (1921-1923)
Calvin Coolidge (1923-1929)*
   vacant (1923-1925)

Charles G. Dawes (1925-1929)
Herbert C. Hoover (1929-1933)
Charles Curtis (1929-1933)
Franklin D. Roosevelt (1933-1945)
John N. Garner (1933-1941)
Henry A. Wallace (1941-1945)
Harry S. Truman (1945)
Harry S. Truman (1945-1953)*
vacant (1945-1949)
Alben W. Barkley (1949-1953)
Dwight D. Eisenhower (1953-1961)
Richard M. Nixon (1953-1961)
John F. Kennedy (1961-1963)
Lyndon B. Johnson (1961-1963)
Lyndon B. Johnson (1963-1969)*
vacant (1963-1965)
Hubert H. Humphrey (1965-1969)
Richard M. Nixon (1969-1974)
Spiro T. Agnew (1969-1973)
Gerald R. Ford (1973-1974)
Gerald R. Ford (1974-1977)*
Nelson A. Rockefeller (1974-1977)
Jimmy Carter (1977-1981)
Walter Mondale (1977-1981)
Ronald Reagan (1981-1989)
George H. W. Bush (1981-1989)
George H. W. Bush (1989-1993)
Danforth Quayle (1989-1993)
William J. Clinton (1993-2001)
Albert Gore, Jr. (1993-2001)
George W. Bush, (2001 -)
Richard Cheney (2001-)

* Indicates succession from the vice presidency to the presidency pursuant to constitutional process.

APPENDIX 2: INSTITUTIONALIZATION OF THE VICE PRESIDENT'S EXECUTIVE OFFICE

As the presiding officer of the Senate, the Vice President has long maintained offices on Capitol Hill. Currently, the Vice President has a ceremonial office in the Capitol and a working office in the Dirksen Office Building.

The institutionalization of the Vice President's executive office began in 1961, when space was provided for the Vice President and his staff in what was then known as the Executive Office Building situated adjacent to the White House.[128] In 1970, Congress established a federal budget line item for the Vice President's executive office in the form of "Special Assistance to the President," as the account is designated. Appropriations are provided "[f]or expenses necessary to enable the Vice President to provide assistance to the President in connection with specially assigned functions."[129] The funds, lately amounting to $3-4 million, allowed the Vice President then, as well as today, to hire qualified staff and to acquire and maintain administrative support.[130] As a consequence, the Vice President not only was relieved from borrowing employees from the departments and agencies to obtain staff assistance, but also was under less compulsion to seek the leadership of temporary study or coordination panels in order to acquire personnel.[131] Soon, staff specialists began to appear, making the Vice President's office a replica, in microcosm, of the President's office. For example, Ford was the first Vice President to have his own national security adviser and his own counsel;[132] Mondale created his own staff for domestic policy development.[133] When a White House staff authorization was legislated in 1978, more detailed vice

---

[128] The Executive Office Building, built in five sections between 1871 and 1888, was initially known as the State, War, and Navy Building, as it housed those three departments. In 1939, with the establishment of the Executive Office of the President, two agencies of this new enclave were located in the State, War, and Navy Building. By 1949, Executive Office agencies completely occupied the structure, and it became known as the Executive Office Building. Later, when a second edifice for Executive Office agencies was constructed on 17th Street, just a short distance from the White House, the original building became known as the Old Executive Office Building. In 1999, the structure was statutorily designated the Dwight D. Eisenhower Executive Office Building, in honor of the 34th President (113 Stat. 1309).

[129] See 84 Stat. 76.

[130] Light, *Vice-Presidential Power*, pp. 69-70, 81-82.

[131] See Ibid., pp. 32-33.

[132] Ibid., pp. 72, 95.

presidential staff employment structure was established, along with more relaxed arrangements for making expenditures for certain authorized expenses incurred by, or in connection with, assisting the Vice President and requirements concerning reimbursements for, and the reporting of, executive branch employees detailed to the Vice President's office.[134]

The Vice President's executive office was formally recognized for the first time in the pages of the *United States Government Organization Manual 1972/73*. The entry, appearing at the end of the section profiling units of the Executive Office of the President (EOP), listed the Vice President's senior assistants and briefly described his constitutional, statutory, and presidentially assigned responsibilities.[135] Amounting to "little more than a symbolic step toward institutionalization," nonetheless, "the listing helped define the boundaries of an executive agency" supporting the President.[136]

During the early months of his tenure, Vice President Ford declined presidential offers of White House staff assistance and began recruiting his own support personnel – a counsel, a national security adviser, speechwriters, and administrative aides. He began with a staff of 17, which, with an appropriations increase, grew to 70 by the time he succeeded to the presidency in August 1974. By one estimate, with these developments, "the Vice President's office became an *independent* source of information and expertise."[137] Ford's personnel practices also established "the Vice President's freedom to hire and fire the staffs of his choice."[138]

The years of the Ford, Rockefeller, and Mondale vice presidencies also saw more formal organization of their offices. "Instead of loose collections of individuals under Humphrey," comments one close observer, "the Ford and Mondale offices became quite hierarchical, involving specific chains of command and functions." As a result, "this tighter organization allowed for better communication between the Vice President's office and the rest of the EOP."[139]

---

[133] Ibid., p. 91.

[134] See 92 Stat. 2446-2448, 2449-2450.

[135] See U.S. General Services Administration, National Archives and Records Service, Office of the Federal Register, *United States Government Organization Manual 1972/73* (Washington: GPO, 1972), p. 89.

[136] Light, *Vice-Presidential Power*, p. 71.

[137] Ibid., pp. 71-72.

[138] Ibid., p. 73.

[139] Ibid., pp. 73, 79-100.

Finally, the Mondale vice presidency brought some other important developments. The first involved perquisites – the availability of "White House mess privileges, better aircraft, better offices, fast printing support, and limousines" – signaling institutional prestige.[140] There was also an integration of the Vice President's staff into the White House policymaking process.[141] Furthermore, Mondale received an office in the West Wing, placing him in close proximity to the Oval Office, to which he was readily welcomed. These developments produced "the rise of an esprit de corps among the Vice President's staff" or, stated another way: "No longer was it the worst moment of a career to work for the Vice President." If nothing else, this new attitude is a reflection of the institutional change that has occurred in the Vice President's executive office, with the result that vice presidential staff "think of themselves as more valuable members of the presidential establishment."[142]

---

[140] Ibid., p. 74.
[141] Ibid., pp. 75-76, 209-210.
[142] Ibid., p. 77.

Chapter 3

VICE PRESIDENTS OF THE UNITED STATES 1789-1933[*]

Charles V. Arja (Editor)

JOHN ADAMS 1ST VICE PRESIDENT: 1789-1797

On April 21, 1789, John Adams, the first vice president of the United States, began his duties as president of the Senate.

Adam's role in the administration of George Washington was sharply constrained by the constitutional limits on the vice-presidency and his own reluctance to encroach upon executive prerogative. He enjoyed a cordial but distant relationship with President Washington, who sought his advice on occasion but relied primarily on the cabinet. Adams played a more active role in the Senate, however, particularly during his first term.

As president of the Senate, Adams cast twenty-nine tie-breaking votes – a record that no successor has ever threatened.[1] His votes protected the

---

[*] Excerpted from Hatfield, Mark O., *Vice Presidents of the United States 1789-1993*, Washington, U.S. Government Printing Office.

[1] Linda Dudik Guerrero, in her study of Adams' vice presidency, found that Adams cast "at least" thirty-one votes, a figure accepted by Adams' most recent biographer. The Senate Historical Office has been able to verify only twenty-nine tie-breaking votes by Adams – still a record, although George Dallas claimed that he cast thirty tie-breaking votes during his vice-presidency. Linda Dudik Guerrero, *John Adams' Vice Presidency, 1789-1797: The Neglected Man in the Forgotten Office* (New York, 1982), p. 128; U.S., Congress, Senate,

president's sole authority over the removal of appointees, influenced the location of the national capital, and prevented war with Great Britain. On at least one occasion he persuaded senators to vote against legislation that he opposed, and he frequently lectured the Senate on procedural and policy matters. Adams' political views and his active role in the Senate made him a natural target for critics of the Washington Administration. Toward the end of his first term, he began to exercise more restraint in the hope of realizing the goal shared by many of his successors: election in his own right as president of the United States.

An avowed supporter of independence in the second Continental Congress, Adams was a member of the committee that prepared the Declaration of Independence. Although Thomas Jefferson of Virginia composed the committee draft, Adams' contribution was no less important. As Jefferson later acknowledged, Adams was the Declaration's "pillar of support on the floor of Congress, its ablest advocate and defender."

Adams took office as vice president on April 21, 1789.[2]

Although Washington rarely consulted Adams on domestic or foreign policy matters, the two men, according to Adams' most recent biographer, John Ferling, "jointly executed many more of the executive branch's ceremonial undertakings than would be likely for a contemporary president and vice-president."[3]

For his own part, Adams professed a narrow interpretation of the vice president's role in the new government. Shortly after taking office, he wrote to his friend and supporter Benjamin Lincoln, "The Constitution has instituted two great offices...and the nation at large has created two officers: one who is the first of the two...is placed at the Head of the Executive, the other at the Head of the Legislative." The following year, he informed another correspondent that the office of the vice president "is totally detached from the executive authority and confined to the legislative."[4]

The Senate 1789-1989, by Robert C. Byrd, S. Doc. 100-20, 100th Cong., 1st sess., vol. 4, *Historical Statistics*, 1789-1992, 1993, p. 640; John Ferling, *John Adams: A Life* (Knoxville, 1992), p. 311.

[2] Linda Grant De Pauw, Charlene Banks Bickford, and LaVonne Marlene Siegel, eds., *Senate Legislative Journal, Documentary History of the First Federal Congress of the United States of America*, vol. 1 (Baltimore, 1972), pp. 21-23.

[3] Ferling, p. 310.

[4] John Adams to Lincoln, May 26, 1789, and John Adams to Hurd, April 5, 1790, quoted in Guerrero, p. 185.

But Adams never *really* considered himself "totally detached" from the executive branch, as the Senate discovered when he began signing legislative documents as "John Adams, Vice President of the United States." Speaking for a majority of the senators, William Maclay of Pennsylvania quickly called Adams to account. "[A]s President of the Senate only can [y]ou sign or authenticate any Act of that body." He lectured the vice president. Uneasy as some senators were at the prospect of having a member of the executive branch preside over their deliberations, they would permit Adams to certify legislation as *president of the Senate, but not as vice president.* Never one to acquiesce cheerfully when he believed that important principles were at stake, Adams struck an awkward compromise, signing Senate documents as "John Adams, Vice President of the United States and President of the Senate."[5]

To the extent that Adams remained aloof from the administration, his stance was as much the result of personality and prudence as of principle. He held the president in high personal esteem and generally deferred to the more forceful Washington as a matter of course.[6] Also, as his biographer Page Smith has explained, the vice president always feared that he would become a "scapegoat for all of Washington's unpopular decision." During the furor over Washington's 1793 proclamation of American neutrality, a weary Adams confided to his wife that he had "held the office of Libellee General long enough."[7]

In the Senate, Adams brought energy and dedication to the presiding officer's chair, but found the task "not quite adapted to my character."[8] Addressing the Senate for the first time on April 21, 1789, he offered the caveat that although "not wholly without experience in public assemblies," he was "more accustomed to take a share of their debates, than to preside in their deliberations." Notwithstanding his lack of experience as a presiding officer, Adams had definite notions regarding the limitations of his office. "It is not for me," he assured the Senate, "to interrupt your deliberations by any general observations on the state of the nation, or by recommending or proposing any particular measures."[9]

---

[5] David P. Currie, "The Constitution in Congress: The First Congress and the Structure of Government, 1789-1791," *University of Chicago Law School Roundtable 2* (1995): 161.

[6] Howe, p. 212; Ferling, p. 310.

[7] Smith, 2:763, 842-43.

[8] Ibid., 2:769.

[9] *Senate Legislative Journal*, pp. 21-23.

Persuaded by Hamilton, Jefferson, and Madison to run for a second term, George Washington was again the obvious and unanimous choice for president. Adams was still the preferred vice-presidential candidate of the New England Federalists, but he faced a serious challenge from Republican candidate George Clinton of New York. Although many of his earlier supporters, including Benjamin Rush, joined the opposition in support of Clinton, Adams won reelection with 77 electoral votes to 50 for Clinton.[10] On March 4, 1793, in the Senate chamber, Washington took the oath of office for a second time. Adams, as always, followed Washington's example but waited until the Third Congress convened on December 2, 1793, to take his second oath of office. No one, apparently, gave much thought to the question of whether or not the nation had a vice president – and a successor Washington, should he die in office or become incapacitated – during the nine-month interval between these two inaugurations.[11]

Early in Adams' second vice-presidential term, France declared war on Great Britain. Washington's cabinet supported the president's policy of neutrality, but its members disagreed over the implementation of that policy. Hamilton urged the president to issue an immediate proclamation of American neutrality; Jefferson warned that only Congress could issue such a declaration and counseled that delaying the proclamation would force concessions from France and England. Recognizing the United States' commercial dependence on Great Britain, Hamilton proposed that the nation conditionally suspend the treaties that granted France access to U.S. ports and guaranteed French possession of the West Indies. Secretary of State Jefferson insisted that the United States honor its treaty obligations. The secretaries similarly disagreed over extending recognition to the emissary of the French republic, "Citizen" Edmond Genêt.

Adams considered absolute neutrality the only prudent course. As a Federalist, he was no supporter of France, but his reluctance to offend a former ally led him to take a more cautious stance than Hamilton. Although Washington sought his advice, Adams scrupulously avoided public comment; he had "no constitutional vote" in the matter and no intention of "taking any side in it or having my name or opinion quoted about it."[12] After the president

---

[10] Miller, p. 96; Smith, 2:826-33.
[11] Stephen W. Stathis and Ronald C. Moe, "America's Other Inauguration," *Presidential Studies Quarterly 10* (Fall 1980): 552.
[12] Miller, Pp. 128-30; Smith, 2:838-44.

decided to recognize Genêt, Adams reluctantly received the controversial Frenchman but predicted that "a little more of this indelicacy and indecency may involve us in a war with all the world."[13]

Although Adams, as vice president, had "no constitutional vote" in the administration's foreign policy, he cast two important tie-breaking foreign policy votes in the Senate, where Republican gains in the 1792 elections had eroded the Federalist majority. In both cases, Adams voted to prevent war with Great Britain and its allies. On March 12, 1794, he voted in favor of an embargo on the domestic sale of vessels and goods seized from friendly nations. The following month, he voted against a bill to suspend American trade with Great Britain.[14] Despite these votes, Adams made every effort to stay aloof from the bitter controversy over foreign policy, remaining silent during the Senate's 1795 debates over the controversial Jay Treaty essential to avert war with Great Britain, but the Federalists still commanded sufficient votes to ratify the treaty without the vice president's assistance.[15]

Vice President Adams addressed the Senate for the last time on February 15, 1797. He thanked current and former members for the "candor and favor" they had extended to him during his eight years as presiding officer. Despite the frustrations and difficulties he had experienced as vice president, Adams left the presiding officer's chair with a genuine regard for the Senate that was in large part mutual. He expressed gratitude to the body for the "uniform politeness" accorded him "from every quarter," and declared that he had "never had the smallest misunderstanding with any member of the Senate." Notwithstanding his earlier pronouncements in favor of a hereditary Senate, Adams assured the members that the "eloquence, patriotism, and independence" that he had witnessed had convinced him that "no council more permanent than this...will be necessary, to defend the rights, liberties, and properties of the people, and to protect the Constitution of the United States."

---

[13] Smith, 2:845.
[14] Miller, p. 154; Smith, 2:853; U.S. Congress, Senate, *Annals of Congress*, 3d Cong., 1st sess., pp. 66, 90.
[15] Smith, 2:873-75; Swanstrom, pp. 120-23.

THOMAS JEFFERSON 2ND VICE PRESIDENT: 1797-1801

Thomas Jefferson entered an ill-defined vice-presidency on March 4, 1797. For guidance on how to conduct himself, he had to rely on a brief reference in the U.S. Constitution, the eight-year experience of John Adams, and his own common sense. Of a profoundly different political and personal temperament from his predecessor, Jefferson knew his performance in that relatively new office would influence its operations well into the future. Unlike Adams, who shared the political beliefs of the president with whom he served, Jefferson and his president belonged to different political parties – a situation that would prove to be unique in all the nation's history. No one who knew the two men expected that Vice President Jefferson would be inclined to serve as President Adams' principal assistant. More likely, he would confine his duties to presiding over the Senate and offering leadership to his anti-administration Republican party in quiet preparation for the election of 1800.[16]

When President Washington announced in September 1796 that he would not run for a third term, a caucus of Federalists in Congress selected Vice President Adams as their presidential candidate. Congressional Republicans turned to Jefferson as the only person capable of defeating Adams, who enjoyed a strong following in New England and was closely associated with the success of the American Revolution.[17] Jefferson had told friends in 1793 that his "retirement from office had meant from all office, high or low,

---

[16] Biographical accounts of Jefferson's life are plentiful and rich. The definitive modern study is Dumas Malone, *Jefferson and His Time*, 6 vols. (Boston, 1948-1981). The volume in that series that covers the years of his vice-presidency is *Jefferson and the Ordeal of Liberty* (Boston, 1962). A first-rate single-volume biography is Noble E. Cunningham, Jr., *In Pursuit of Reason: The Life of Thomas Jefferson* (Baton Rouge, 1987). For the period of Jefferson's vice-presidency, see Noble E. Cunningham, Jr., *The Jeffersonian Republicans: The Formation of Party Organization, 1789-1801* (Chapel Hill, 1957). For a series of twenty-five excellent essays that focus on each of Jefferson's "extraordinary collection of talents," see Merrill D. Peterson, ed., *Thomas Jefferson: A Reference Biography* (New York, 1986). This work also contains a comprehensive bibliography. There are several major collections of Jefferson's writing, including Paul Leicester Ford, *The Writings of Thomas Jefferson*, 10 vols. (New York, 1892-1899) and the more comprehensive, but as yet incomplete, Julian P. Boyd, et al., eds., *The Papers of Thomas Jefferson* (1950-). The latter work has appeared to date only to the mid-1970s and thus is of no assistance for the vice-presidential period. One volume associated with this massive project, however, is of direct value; appearing as part of the project's "Second Series" is Wilbur Samuel Howell, ed., *Jefferson's Parliamentary Writings: 'Parliamentary Pocket-Book' and A Manual of Parliamentary Practice* (Princeton, 1988).

[17] Malone, *Jefferson and the Ordeal of Liberty*, pp. 274-75.

without exception."[18] While he continued to hold those views in 1796, he reluctantly allowed Republican leader Madison to advance his candidacy – in part to block the ambitions of his archrival, Alexander Hamilton.

As part of a strategy to erode Jefferson's southern support, the Federalists selected as Adams' running mate Thomas Pinckney of South Carolina, author of the popular 1795 treaty with Spain.[19] Hamilton, Adam's bitter rival within the Federalist Party, encouraged Federalist electors in the North to give both their votes to Adams and Pinckney. On the safe assumption that Pinckney would draw more votes than Adams from the other regions, and recognizing that Jefferson lacked support north and east of the Delaware River, Hamilton mistakenly concluded this tactic would assure Pinckney's election.[20] Adams' supporters countered Hamilton's plan by convincing a number of their party's electors to vote for someone other than Pinckney. As a result, Adams won the presidency with 71 of a possible 138 electoral votes. But Jefferson with 68 votes, rather than Pinckney with 59 votes, became vice president. Aaron Burr, the Republican vice-presidential contender, received only 30 votes, while 48 other votes were scattered among nine minor candidates.[21] This election produced the first and only mixed-party presidential team in the nation's history.

Not looking forward to reentering the political fray and feeling unprepared to assume presidential responsibilities for foreign policy at a time when relations with European nations were strained, Jefferson may have been the only person in the history of American politics to celebrate the fact that he lost a presidential election.

Adams and Jefferson started off cordially. The Virginian, having enjoyed Adams' friendship in the second Continental Congress and while in retirement at Monticello, set out to forge a good public relationship with him as his vice president. Although he realized that they would probably disagree on many issues, Jefferson deeply respected Adams' prior service to the nation.[22]

On the eve of their inauguration, Adams and Jefferson met briefly to discuss the possibility of sending Jefferson to France as part of a three-member delegation to calm the increasingly turbulent relations between the

---

[18] Quoted in Cunningham, "The Jeffersonian Republican Party," p. 249.

[19] Ibid., p. 274.

[20] Ibid., p. 278.

[21] *Congressional Quarterly's Guide to U.S. Elections*, 3d ed. (Washington, 1994), p. 361.

[22] Ibid., p. 293; Cunningham, *In Pursuit of Reason*, pp. 206-7; Ferling, *John Adams: A Life* (Knoxville, 1992), pp. 332-34.

two countries. When the two men concluded that this would be an improper role for the vice president, they agreed on substituting Jefferson's political ally, James Madison. The bond between president and vice president seemed – for the moment – particularly close.

Several days after the inauguration, Jefferson encountered the president at a dinner party. He took the opportunity to report that Madison was not interested in the diplomatic mission to France. Adams replied that, in any event, he would not have been able to select Madison because of pressure from within his cabinet to appoint a Federalist. This confirmed Jefferson's view that the new president lacked his own political compass and was too easily swayed by partisan advisers. Thereafter, Adams never consulted Jefferson on an issue of national significance.[23] For his part, the vice president turned exclusively to his political role as leader of the Republicans and to his governmental duty as the Senate's presiding officer.

While in Philadelphia to commence his vice-presidential duties, Jefferson acceded to a second leadership position – the presidency of the American Philosophical Society. Conveniently located near Congress Hall, this august scientific and philosophical body counted among its previous leaders Benjamin Franklin and mathematician David Rittenhouse. Jefferson attained the post on the strength of his *Notes on the State of Virginia* (first English edition, 1787), which secured his reputation as a preeminent scholar and scientist and is today considered "the most important scientific work published in America in the eighteenth century."

Deteriorating relations with France preoccupied the government during Jefferson's vice-presidency and fostered anti-French sentiment at home. No one event caused the conflict, but a decree of the ruling Directory and a series of French proposals fueled the spreading fire. The decree declared that neutral ships with English merchandise or commodities could be seized. Congress, in turn, sought to protect American commerce by authorizing the arming of private vessels.

In what proved to be a futile attempt to improve relations, President Adams sent three envoys to France. When they reached Paris in October 1797, however, the French government refused to receive them until they satisfied requirements that the Americans considered insulting. Minor French officials – publicly labeled "X, Y, and Z" – met with the envoys and presented

---

[23] Malone, *Jefferson and the Ordeal of Liberty*, p. 299.

proposals that included a request for a $12 million loan and a $250,000 bribe in exchange for recognition of the United States and the establishment of formal ties. Despite his sympathies for France, Jefferson viewed the proposals as a supreme insult, yet he understood that a war could undermine the nation's newly set constitutional foundations and strengthen the pro-British Federalist leadership.

The publication in April 1798 of what became known as the "XYZ papers" produced widespread anger and created a frenzied atmosphere in which overzealous patriotism flourished. In an effort to restore their party's popularity, Federalist legislators – recently the targets of public scorn for their support of the unpopular Jay treaty with England – seized on the anti-French hostility that the XYZ affair had generated. Federalists in Congress, their numbers expanded in response to public anger against France, quickly passed a series of tough measures to set the nation on a war footing. Most notorious of these statutes were the Sedition Act, the Naturalization Act, and the Alien Act, all viewed by their Republican opponents as distinctly partisan measures to curtail individual rights.[24]

The Senate approved the Sedition Act on July 4, 1798, in the final days of the Fifth Congress after Jefferson had left for Virginia. The statute curtailed the rights of Americans to criticize their government and provided punishment for any person writing, uttering, or publishing "any false, scandalous and malicious writing" against the president or Congress with the intent of inflaming public passions against them.[25] The Federalists immediately invoked the law's provisions to suppress Republican criticism.

Thomas Jefferson's *Manual of Parliamentary Practice* is, without question, the distinguishing feature of his vice-presidency. The single greatest contribution to the Senate by any person to serve as vice president, it is as relevant to the Senate of the late twentieth century as it was to the Senate of the late eighteenth century. Reflecting the *Manual's* continuing value, the Senate in 1993 provided for its publication in a special edition to commemorate the 250th anniversary of Jefferson's birth.

Jefferson had conceived the idea of a parliamentary manual as he prepared to assume the duties of the vice-presidency early in 1797. John Adams offered an inadequate model for the role of presiding officer, for he had earned a reputation for officious behavior in the Senate president's chair. To avoid the

---

[24] Malone, *Jefferson and the Ordeal of Liberty*, chapter XXIV.

criticism that attended Adams' performance, Jefferson believed the Senate's presiding officer needed to follow "some known system of rules, that he may neither leave himself free to indulge caprice or passion, nor open to the imputation of them."[26] The lack of carefully delineated rules, he feared, would make the Senate prone to the extremes of chaos and tyranny. He was particularly concerned about the operation of Senate Rule 16, which provided that the presiding officer was to be solely responsible for deciding all questions of order, "without debate and without appeal."

Jefferson compiled his *Manual of Parliamentary Practice* during the course of his four-year vice-presidency. He designed it to contain guidance for the Senate drawn from "the precepts of the Constitution, the regulations of the Senate, and where these are silent, the rules of Parliament." The *Manual*, loaded with references to British parliamentary authorities, contained fifty-three sections devoted to such topics as privileges, petitions, motions, resolutions, bills, treaties, conferences, and impeachments.

Jefferson's *Manual* was first published in 1801, shortly after he became president. A second edition followed in 1812, and in 1837 the House of Representatives established that the rules listed in the *Manual* would "govern the House in all cases to which they are applicable and in which they are not inconsistent with the standing rules and orders of the House and the joint rules of the Senate."[27] Although the *Manual* has not been treated as "a direct authority on parliamentary procedure in the Senate,"[28] it is the Senate that today more closely captures Jefferson's ideal of a genuinely deliberative body.

---

[25] 1 Stat. 596-597.

[26] Thomas Jefferson, *A Manual of Parliamentary Practice for the Use of the Senate of the United States*, in The Papers of Thomas Jefferson, Second Series, *Jefferson's Parliamentary Writings*, Wilbur Samuel Howell, ed., p. 355. Howell has produced the definitive scholarly edition of Jefferson's *Manual* (pp. 339-444).

[27] The Senate has regularly published that work as a companion to the body's formal rules. The *Manual* was included as a section within the *Senate Manual* from 1886 to 1975 and was republished in 1993, on the occasion of the 250th anniversary of Jefferson's birth, in the original 1801 edition. Some practices discussed in Jefferson's *Manual* set core precedents that the Senate has followed ever since, although the work is not considered a direct authority on procedure. The *Manual's* influence quickly extended beyond domestic legislature, as editors translated the work into other languages. At least 143 editions have been printed. The work has abetted self-government in countries as far away as the Philippines, where over one hundred years later it was adopted as a supplementary guide in that nation's senate and House of Representatives.

[28] U.S. Congress, Senate, Riddick's *Senate Procedure: Precedents and Practices*, by Floyd M. Riddick and Alan S. Frumin, S. Doc. 101-28, 101st Cong., 1st sess., p. 754.

Thomas Jefferson infused the vice-presidency with his genius through the contribution of his *Manual of Parliamentary Practice* – a magisterial guide to legislative procedure that has retained its broad utility through two centuries. He also contributed to the office his example of skillful behind-the-scenes legislative leadership, and he offered a philosophical compass on the issues of constitutionalism and individual rights. Biographer Dumas Malone provides a final analysis of Jefferson's style as party leader during his vice-presidential tenure.

AARON BURR 3RD VICE PRESIDENT: 1801-1805

None of Aaron Burr's contemporaries knew quite what to make of this complex and fascinating individual. As Senator Robert C. Byrd observed in his November 13, 1987, address on the life and career of this controversial vice president, "there is much that we will never know about the man."

Burr was one of the most maligned and mistrusted public figures of his era – and, without question, the most controversial vice president of the early republic – but he never attempted to justify or explain his actions to his friends or to his enemies. One editor of Burr's papers has lamented, "Almost alone among the men who held high office in the early decades of this nation, Burr left behind no lengthy recriminations against his enemies…no explanations and justifications for his actions." He seems to have cared very little what his contemporaries thought of him, or how historians would judge him.[29] Few figures in American history have been as vilified, or as romanticized, by modern writers.[30] Urbane and charming, generous beyond prudence, proud, shrewd, and ambitious, he stood apart from other public figures of his day.

In 1800, Republican strategists hoped to cement their fledgling coalition by seeking, for geographical balance, a New Yorker as their vice-presidential candidate. One obvious choice was New York's elder statesman, George

---

[29] Mary-Jo Kline, "Aaron Burr as a Symbol of Corruption in the New Republic," in *Before Watergate: Problems of Corruption in American Society*, ed. Abraham S. Eisenstadt, Ari Hoogenboom and Hans L. Trefousse (Brooklyn, NY, 1978), p. 74. Mary-Jo Kline and Joanne Wood Ryan's two-volume letterpress edition of Burr's public papers, published by Princeton University Press in 1983, is an invaluable resource for scholars.

[30] See, for example, Samuel H. Wandell, *Aaron Burr in Literature: Books, Pamphlets, Periodicals, and Miscellany Relating to Aaron Burr and His Leading Political Contemporaries* (Port Washington, NY, 1972; reprint of 1936 edition).

Clinton, but his reluctance to enter the race[31] cleared the way for Burr's unanimous nomination by the Republican caucus on May 11, 1800. Although Jefferson would later claim – after Burr discredited himself by his behavior during the election and in office – that he had harbored reservations about his New York lieutenant form the time of their first meeting in 1791 or 1792, contemporary correspondence suggests that their relationship was cordial during the 1790s. If Jefferson had reservations about Burr in 1800, he laid them aside to secure a Republican victory, using his influence to ensure that all of Virginia's twenty-one electors would cast their second votes for his running mate.

Jefferson soon had ample reason to distrust Burr. In 1800, as in the three previous presidential elections, each elector cast two votes without distinguishing between presidential and vice-presidential candidates. Republican strategists expected that all of their electors would cast one vote for Jefferson and that most – enough to guarantee that Burr would receive the second highest number of votes but not enough to jeopardize Jefferson's margin – would cast their second votes for Burr. Jefferson and his lieutenants left the implementation of this scheme to chance, never asking even a single elector to withhold a vote from Burr, although Jefferson's friend and adviser, James Madison, would later allege that Republicans had been lulled by "false assurances dispatched at the critical moment to the electors of one state, that the votes of another would be different form what they proved to be."

As soon as the outcome of the election became apparent, but before Congress met to count the electoral votes on February 11, 1801, the Federalists began a last-ditch effort to defeat Jefferson. Some, while resigned to a Republican victory, believed that the less partisan and more flexible Burr was by far the lesser of two evils. Others supported Burr in the hope that, if a deadlock could be prolonged indefinitely, the Federalist-dominated Congress could resolve the impasse with legislation authorizing the Senate to elect a Federalist president – a hope that had no constitutional basis but demonstrated the uncertain temper of the times. Alexander Hamilton, a prominent New York Federalist, actively opposed Burr, repeatedly attempting to convince his colleagues that Burr as a man whose "public principles have no other spring or aim than his own aggrandizement."[32]

---

[31] See page 56 of this volume, "George Clinton".

[32] Malone, *Jefferson and the Ordeal of Liberty*, pp. 489-96; Parmet and Hecht, pp. 158-60; Cunningham, "Election of 1800," pp. 131-32.

Burr never explained his role in the drama that subsequently unfolded in the House of Representatives, which cast thirty-six ballots before finally declaring Jefferson the winner on February 17, 1801. The election and the confusion that followed, exposed a critical flaw in the constitutional provision governing the election of the president and the vice president. The Twelfth Amendment, which passed both houses during the fall of 1803 and was ratified by the requisite number of states in time for the 1804 election, changed the method of election by requiring electors to designate one vote for a presidential candidate and the other for a vice-presidential candidate. Intended to prevent an unscrupulous vice-presidential candidate (or his supporters) from subverting the electoral process.

Burr was one of the most skilled parliamentarians to serve as president of the Senate, a striking contrast to Adams and a worthy successor to Jefferson. "Mr. Burr, the Vice President, presides in the Senate with great ease, dignity & propriety," Senator William Plumer (F-NH) observed. "He preserves good order, silence - & decorum in debate – he confines the speaker to the point. He has excluded all spectators from the area of the Senate chamber, except the members from the other House. A measure which contributes much to good order."[33]

But, although Burr was universally respected for his parliamentary skills and his impartial rulings, Senate Republicans noted with mounting concern his easy familiarity with his many Federalist friends. Alienated from his own party, pragmatic at the expense of principle, and beset by the chronic financial difficulties that dogged him throughout his career, Burr was increasingly regarded by his fellow Republicans as an unprincipled opportunist who would stop at nothing to rebuild his shattered political and personal fortunes.[34] They found ample evidence of the vice president's apostasy on January 27, 1802, when Burr cast a tie-breaking vote that undercut the Republican effort to repeal the Judiciary Act of 1801.

That act, signed into law less than a week before Jefferson's election, enacted badly need reforms, providing circuit court judges to relieve the Supreme Court justices from the burdensome and exhausting chore of riding circuit, and reducing the number of justices form six to five, effective with the next vacancy. The act became effective in time to allow John Adams to

---

[33] Brown, pp. 74-75.

[34] Kline, "Aaron Burr as a Symbol of Corruption in the New Republic," pp. 69-76; Parmet and Hecht, pp. 168-93.

appoint Federalist judges to the new circuit courts, a development that heightened Republican fears of a Federalist-controlled judiciary. And, with one less Supreme Court justice, it appeared unlikely that Jefferson would ever have an opportunity to appoint a Republican nominee to the Supreme Court. On January 6, 1802, Senator John Breckinridge (R-KY) introduced a bill to repeal the Judiciary Act. Burr's vote would prove crucial in the Senate, where the absence of one Republican and the resignation of another had eroded the administration's already slim majority. Republican were greatly relieved when the Senate deadlocked on a vote to proceed to a third reading of the repeal bill on January 26, and Burr resolved the tie in favor of the repealers. But he had secretly informed Federalists that he would support their attempts to block repeal by adding amendments that would make the Judiciary Act acceptable to moderate Republicans. Thus, the next day, when his friend Jonathan Dayton (F-NJ) moved to refer the bill to "a select committee, with instructions to consider and report the alterations which may be proper in the Judiciary system of the United States," Burr resolved the tie in favor of the Federalists.

Burr soon abandoned any hope of winning re-nomination to a second term. In early 1804, he called on Jefferson to inform him that he recognized "it would be for the interest of the republican cause for him to retire; that a disadvantageous schism would otherwise take place." The Republicans ultimately settled on George Clinton as their new vice-presidential candidate. Burr retired from national politics, without Jefferson's "mark of favor," entering the 1804 New York gubernatorial race in a desperate attempt to restore his rapidly failing career.

Burr no longer commanded the respect and support from New York Republicans that he had once enjoyed. He entered the gubernatorial race as an independent and actively sought Federalist support when it became apparent that the Federalists would not offer a candidate of their own. But Alexander Hamilton was soon "intriguing for any candidate who can have a chance of success against A.B." Burr plunged enthusiastically into the campaign, delivering speeches and distributing campaign literature, but he could not overcome the liabilities he had acquired since 1800. He lost the election by an overwhelming 8,000-vote margin.[35]

Burr's defeat left him bitter and disillusioned. He blamed Hamilton for his predicament, and when he learned that his rival and former ally had referred to him as a "dangerous man, and who ought not to be trusted," he demanded an explanation. The conflict escalated, as Burr and Hamilton exchanged a series of letters, and finally came to a head on June 27, 1804, when Burr challenged Hamilton to a duel. The grim engagement took place on July 11 at Weehawken, New Jersey, and resulted in Hamilton's death the following day.[36]

Burr's opponents called for his arrest, but the outcry against him was by no means universal. Dueling was expressly prohibited by law in most states, and murder was a crime in every state. But encounters on the "field of honor" still took place during the early nineteenth century, particularly in the southern states. Burr had previously challenged Hamilton's brother-in-law, John Church, to a duel – a bloodless encounter that enabled them to confront and then forget their differences – and Hamilton's son, Philip, had incurred a moral wound on the dueling ground the previous year. Henry Clay, Andrew Jackson, and others of similar stature subscribed to the Code Duello, but few suffered the stigma that Burr carried after that fatal morning at Weehawken. He left New York a month after Hamilton's death to allow "public opinion" to "take its proper course."

Burr's final days in the Senate would have been unpleasant even without the strain of presiding over a taxing and bitterly contested impeachment trial. He presided over the February 13, 1805 joint session of Congress, counting the electoral returns. In that capacity, he announced that Jefferson had been reelected and that his old rival, George Clinton, would succeed him as vice president. Senator Samuel Mitchell reported that Burr performed this "painful duty" with "so much regularity and composure that you would not have see the least deviation from his common manner, or heard the smallest departure from his usual tone."

The forty-nine-year-old former vice president was heavily in debt at the time of his forced retirement from politics. He had been involved in a number of speculative ventures throughout his career, many of which had resulted in substantial losses. Generous beyond prudence, Burr could never refuse a relative or a friend in need, even if it meant going further into debt.

Snubbed by many of his former acquaintances and wholly removed from the "game of politics" that had once been his joy and delight, Burr followed

---

[35] Parmet and Hecht, pp. 194-201; Kline, "Aaron Burr as a Symbol of Corruption in the New Republic," pp. 72-73.
[36] Parmet and Hecht, pp. 194-215.

the independence movements that were changing the face of Latin America with a lively but cautious interest. In 1829, he petitioned the government for a pension based on his military service during the Revolution, a crusade that continued until his plea was finally granted in 1834. He became progressively more eccentric and impoverished as the years passed. In 1831, William Seward found him living in a dirty garret, shabbily dressed but optimistic as ever. Incapacitated by a series of strokes in 1834, Burr lived on the charity of friends and relatives until his death at Port Richmond, Staten Island, on September 14, 1836. During his final hours, a clergyman inquired about his prospects for salvation. Evasive and cryptic to the end, Burr only replied, "On that subject I am coy."

GEORGE CLINTON 4TH VICE PRESIDENT: 1805-1812

George Clinton took office as the nation's fourth vice president on March 4, 1805. He was the second vice president to serve under Thomas Jefferson, having replaced fellow New Yorker Aaron Burr whose intransigence in 1800 had nearly cost Jefferson the presidency. A Revolutionary War hero who had served as governor of New York for two decades, Clinton seemed an ideal choice to supplant Burr while preserving the New York-Virginia alliance that formed the backbone of the Republican coalition.

Clinton was, in the words of a recent biographer, "an enigma." The British forces that torched Kingston, New York, during the Revolution, as well as the 1911 conflagration that destroyed most of Clinton's papers at the New York Public Library, have deprived modern researchers of sources that might have illuminated his personality and explained his motives.[37] Much of the surviving evidence, however, coupled with the observations of Clinton's contemporaries, support historian Alan Taylor's assessment that "Clinton crafted a masterful, compelling public persona...[T]hat...masked and permitted an array of contradictions that would have ruined a lesser, more transparent politician."[38] He was, in Taylor's view, "The astutest politician in Revolutionary New York," a man who "understood the power of symbolism and the new popularity of a plain style especially when practiced by a man

---

[37] Kaminski, p. 1.
[38] Alan Taylor, review of Kaminski, George Clinton, *Journal of the Early Republic 13* (Fall 1993): 414-15.

with the means and accomplishments to set himself above the common people."[39]

Clinton emerged as one of the most prominent opponents of the new Constitution. Widely respected for his heroism during the war and for his devotion to Republican principles, George Clinton was a candidate who could replace Burr without alienating New York voters. His age and precarious health were important considerations for Jefferson, who calculated that in 1808 the sixty-five-year-old hero would be too old to challenge his intended successor, Secretary of State James Madison, for the Republican presidential nomination.

After the election, Clinton was all but shunted aside by a president who had no wish to enhance his vice president's stature in the administration or encourage his presidential ambitions. Nor was he an effective presiding officer. Senator Plumer observed, when Clinton assumed the presiding officer's chair on December 16, 1805, that he seemed "altogether unacquainted" with the Senate's rules, had a "clumsy awkward way of putting a question," and "Preserves little or no order."[40] Senator John Quincy Adams (F-MA) shared Plumer's concern. The Senate's new president was "totally ignorant of all the most common forms of proceeding in the Senate," he wrote in his diary. "His judgment is neither quick no strong: so there is no more dependence upon the correctness of his determination from his understanding than from his experience...a worse choice than Mr. Clinton could scarcely have been made."

ELBRIDGE GERRY 5TH VICE PRESIDENT: 1813-1814

The vice-presidency had been vacant for nearly a year by the time Elbridge Gerry took office as the nation's fifth vice president on March 4, 1813. His predecessor, George Clinton, an uncompromising "Old Republican" with frustrated presidential ambitions, had died in office on April 20, 1812. Clinton's constant carping about President James Madison's foreign policy had put him at odds with the administration. Gerry, who replaced Clinton as the Republican vice-presidential nominee in the 1812 election, was a vice

---

[39] Alan Taylor, *William Cooper's Town: Power and Persuasion on the Frontier of the Early American Republic* (New York, 1995), p. 156.
[40] Brown, pp. 348-49.

president more to Madison's liking. An enthusiastic supporter of Jefferson's embargo and Madison's foreign policy, he offered a welcome contrast to the independent-minded and cantankerous New Yorker who had proved so troublesome during the president's first term. But, like Clinton, Gerry would die in office before the end of his term, leaving Madison – and the nation – once again without a vice president.

One of four delegates chosen by the Massachusetts legislature to attend the 1787 Constitutional Convention, Gerry was, in his biographer's words, "one of the most active participants in the entire Convention."[41] A member of the moderate bloc – he was neither an extreme nationalist nor a committed states' rights advocate – he acted as a conciliator during the first phases of the convention. As chair of the committee that resolved the impasse between the large and small states over representation in the national legislature, Gerry made several impassioned speeches in support of the "Great Compromise," which provided for equal representation of the states in the Senate and proportional representation in the House of Representatives.[42]

Madison had other plans for Gerry. With the 1812 presidential election fast approaching and the vice-presidency vacant since George Clinton's death in April, Madison was more anxious to find a suitable running mate than to fill a customs post. He preferred a candidate who would attract votes in the New England states yet would not threaten the succession of the "Virginia dynasty" in the 1816 election. Former Senator John Langdon of New Hampshire, the party's first choice, was too old and too ill to accept the nomination. After he declined, the Republican caucus turned to the sixty-seven-year-old Gerry, a choice that Madison approved despite Albert Gallatin's prediction that the Massachusetts patriot "would give us as much trouble as our late Vice-President." Gerry had supported Jefferson's embargo and Madison's foreign policy, remaining steadfast after the United States declared war against Great Britain in June 1812. Like Madison, he believed that the war was necessary to protect the liberties that both men had labored so hard to secure during the Revolution.[43]

---

[41] Billias, p. 158; Ralph Ketcham, James Ketcham, *James Madison: A Biography* (Charlottesville, VA, 1992; reprint of 1971 edition), p. 194.

[42] Billias, pp. 153-84. Ketcham, p. 523; Norman K. Risjord, "Election of 1812," in History of American Presidential Elections, 1789-1968, edited by Arthur M. Schlesinger, Jr. and Fred L. Israel, vol. 1 (New York, 1971), p. 252.

[43] According to Madison scholar Robert Allen Rutland, the president believed that "war with Britain would reaffirm the commitment of 1776." Robert Allen Rutland, *The Presidency of*

DANIEL D. TOMPKINS 6TH VICE PRESIDENT: 1817-1825

Daniel D. Thompkins was by all accounts an exceptionally handsome individual. He had a "face of singular masculine beauty," one essayist noted, and a "gentile, polished and unpretentious" demeanor. Thompkins' biographer discovered that "almost every noted American artist" of the time painted the handsome New York Republican,[44] and the images reproduced in Raymond Irwin's study of Tompkins' career depict an attractive and obviously self-confident young politician. John Trumbull's 1809 portrait, for example, shows Tompkins as he appeared during his first term as governor of New York: a carefully dressed, poised, and seemingly contented public man, his dark hair framing an even-featured and not-yet-careworn face.[45]

But had Trumbull painted Tompkins in 1825, the year he retired from public life after two terms as vice president during James Monroe's administration, he would have captured a vastly different likeness. A decade of financial privation and heavy drinking, coupled with accusations that he had mishandled state and federal funds while serving as governor of New York during the War of 1812, had prematurely aged Tompkins. He was, at the age of fifty, an embittered and tortured old man, his once-promising career brought to an untimely end. "There was a time when no man in the state dared compete with him for any office in the gift of the people." A contemporary reflected after Tompkins' death on June 11, 1825, "and his habits of intemperance alone prevented him from becoming President of the United States."[46]

Tompkins' able and energetic leadership during the war made him one of the best-loved men in his state. One of his aides, novelist Washington Irving, pronounced him "absolutely on of the worthiest men I ever knew...honest, candid, prompt, indefatigable,"[47] a sentiment that many shared. The editor of the *Albany Argus* suggested in January 1816 that "if private worth – if public

---

James Madison (Lawrence, KS, 1990), p. 97. Gerry elaborated his sentiments in his May 24, 1813, inaugural address. U.S., Congress, Senate, *Annuals of Congress*, 13th Cong., 2d sess., pp. 10-13.

[44] Irwin, pp. 59, 227.

[45] Reproduced in ibid., facing p. 66.

[46] Philip Hone, quoted in ibid., p. 309.

[47] Washington Irving to William Irving, October 14, 1814, quoted in Pierre M. Irving, ed., *The Life and Letters of Washington Irving*, vol. 1 (Detroit, 1967; reprint of 1863 edition), pp. 320-21.

service – if fervent patriotism and practical talents are to be regarded in selecting a President then Governor Tompkins stands forth to the nation with unrivalled pretensions."[48] Republicans in the state legislature endorsed him as their presidential candidate on February 14, 1816, and a week later he was re-nominated as the party's gubernatorial candidate. Tompkins defeated Federalist Rufus King by a comfortable margin in the gubernatorial race after an intensely partisan campaign focusing on the candidates' wartime records. But the victory was marred by Federalist accusations that Governor Tompkins had misused public monies during the war, charges that would haunt him for the remainder of his life.[49]

JOHN C. CALHOUN 7TH VICE PRESIDENT: 1825-1832

John C. Calhoun assumed office as the nation's seventh vice president on March 4, 1825, during a period of extraordinary political ferment. The demise of the Federalist Party after the War of 1812 had not, as former President James Monroe had hoped, ushered in an "Era of Good Feelings," free from party divisions. Contrary to Monroe's expectations, the partisan strife of earlier years had not abated during his two terms as president but had, instead, infected the Republican Party, which had declined into a broad-based but rapidly disintegrating coalition of disparate elements. Five individuals, all of them Republicans, had entered the 1824 presidential contest, one of the most controversial and bitterly contested races in the nation's history. The "National Republicans," group that included Calhoun, House Speaker Henry Clay, and Secretary of State John Quincy Adams, supported an expansive, nationalist agenda; the "Radicals," allies of Treasury Secretary William Crawford, were strict constructionists and advocates of limited government. Other Republicans had rallied to the standard of Andrew Jackson, a former Tennessee senator and the military hero whose stunning victory at the Battle of New Orleans had salvaged the nation's pride during the War of 1812.

Calhoun, who presided over the Senate at the dawning of its Golden Age, had reached the height of his career. Given his meteoric rise to national prominence as a talented young congressman during the War of 1812 and his solid record of accomplishment as secretary of war during Monroe's

---

[48] Quoted in Irwin, pp. 197-98.
[49] Ibid., pp. 197-205.

administration, he had every reason to assume that he would one day become president.

Calhoun served in the House until 1817. Sobered by the nation's near-defeat during the War of 1812, he continued his interest in military affairs, opposing troop reductions and advocating the establishment of two additional service academies. As his modern biographer has observed, Calhoun "equated defense with national self-sufficiency." Toward that end, he accepted protective tariffs and helped draft legislation to establish the Second Bank of the United States in 1816. Concerned that the nation's interior settlements lacked the roads and other improvements that he believed essential to economic development and national security, he proposed legislation to earmark for internal improvements the $1.5 million charter fee the bank paid to the federal government, as well as the yields of government-owned bank stocks.[50]

On June 4, 1826, Calhoun notified Andrew Jackson that he would support his 1828 presidential bid. Calhoun, with his disciplined intellect and rigid sense of propriety, presented a striking contrast to the popular and dashing military hero. The two were never close, and Calhoun never completely trusted Jackson. In fact, several years earlier, while serving on Monroe's cabinet, the South Carolinian had urged the president to discipline Jackson for his unauthorized invasion of Spanish Florida during the Seminole War.[51] But Calhoun needed time to recoup his political fortunes, and Jackson had vowed to serve but a single term if elected president. The old hero welcomed Calhoun's support, assuring him that they would "march hand in hand in their [the people's] cause," cementing one of the most ill starred partnerships in the history of the vice-presidency.[52]

Calhoun's second vice-presidential term was even more of an ordeal than his first. His suspicions that Jackson might pose as great a threat to popular liberties as his predecessor were soon confirmed. The president failed to repudiate the tariff – clear evidence that he had fallen under Van Buren's spell – and his appointment of the "Little Magician" as secretary of state boded will

---

[50] Charles Sellers, The Market Revolution: Jacksonian America, 1815-1846 (New York, 1991), pp. 76-79; Peterson, p. 49; Niven, pp. 51-57. President James Madison vetoed the "Bonus Bill" on Constitutional grounds.

[51] John C. Calhoun to Andrew Jackson, June 4, 1826, Calhoun Papers, 10:110-11; Peterson, pp. 151-52; Niven, pp. 68-71, 119-21.

[52] Harry L. Watson, Liberty and Power: The Politics of Jacksonian America (New York, 1990), pp. 73-74.

for Calhoun. The vice president was soon isolated within an administration where Van Buren and his protectionist allies appeared to be gaining and upper hand.[53]

Calhoun returned to the Senate in November 1845 and remained there for the rest of his life. Increasingly defensive about the institution of slavery as the abolition movement gained momentum, and agitated at the growing discord between the slaveholding and free states, he spoke, as he informed the Senate in 1847, as "a Southern man and a slaveholder." As secretary of state Calhoun had strongly supported the annexation of Texas. After Pennsylvania Representative David Wilmot offered his famous proviso as an amendment to an administration war bill, however, the South Carolina senator realized that the acquisition of additional territory would inevitably heighten the sectional conflict over slavery. The Wilmot Proviso, which would have barred slavery from all lands acquired from Mexico, pushed Calhoun into the anti-administration camp. He vehemently opposed the war policy of President James K. Polk, warning that the acquisition of Mexican territory, with its population of "pure Indians and by far the larger portion of the residue mixed blood," would corrupt the nation's culture and institutions.[54]

Calhoun died on March 31, 1850, convinced that his beloved South would one day withdraw from the Union he had labored so long and hard to strengthen and preserve.

MARTIN VAN BUREN 8TH VICE PRESIDENT: 1833-1837

Few people ever really knew Martin Van Buren. The impeccable attire, ready wit, and unfailing tact that set him apart from his contemporaries masked a nagging sense of insecurity that dogged him throughout his political career. His father, a tavern keeper of modest means, had been able to provide him with only a rudimentary education. One of Van Buren's better-educated associates observed that his "knowledge of books outside of his profession was more limited than that of any other public man" he had ever known and that Van Buren never prepared a state paper without asking a friend to "revise and correct that document."

---

[53] Niven, pp. 165-69.
[54] Ibid., pp. 295-313.

Reviled as a "schemer" and a master "manipulator" by contemporaries who lacked (and probably envied) his uncanny political acumen, he was known throughout his career by an unparalleled assortment of nicknames, none of them entirely favorable. But "the Little Magician" (also known as "the American Talleyrand," "the Red Fox of Kinderhook," the "Mistletoe Politician," and by a variety of other sobriquets)[55] left a solid record of accomplishment that few of his better-known fellows could rival. More than any other individual of his time, Van Buren realized the importance of party organization, discipline, and political patronage. He engineered Andrew Jackson's victory in the 1828 presidential election and later became a trusted confidant and adviser to "Old Hickory," a relationship that continued after Van Buren became vice president in 1833. No previous vice president enjoyed a greater measure of influence that Van Buren, and no vice president, in over three decades, had assumed that office as the "heir apparent."

Jackson won an impressive victory in 1828, widely heralded as a triumph of the "common man." Writing his *Autobiography* many years after the fact, Van Buren attributed the outcome of this historic election to the "zealous union between that portion of the republican party who ...had shown themselves willing to sacrifice personal preferences to its harmony, the numerous supporters of Gen. Jackson...and the friends of Mr. Calhoun...strengthened by the mismanagement of the administration." Van Buren achieved a personal victory as well, winning election as governor of New York. But he served less than two months of this position, resigning to accept an appointment as secretary of state in the new administration.[56]

Jackson had every reason to rejoice at the outcome of the election. The voters had, he believed, given him a mandate to destroy the bank, and he was rid of Calhoun. In Van Buren, Jackson had a vice president more to his liking. Old Hickory respected his second vice president and seems to have felt sincere affection for him, as well. Some longtime Jackson cronies were deeply jealous of the New Yorker, who, as one critic put it, stuck "close to the President as a blistering plaster."[57] But Van Buren was not, as critics of both men so frequently alleged, the "power-behind-the-throne." Jackson was a formidable tactician in his own right and a man of resolute convictions, fully capable of

---

[55] Schlesinger, p. 49; Carl Sifakis, *The Dictionary of Historic Nicknames* (New York, 1984), p. 508.

[56] Fitzpatrick, ed., 1:220-24.

[57] Remini, *Jackson and the Course of American Democracy*, p. 46.

determining his own course of action. Van Buren was not his only confidant; throughout his two terms as president, Jackson also relied on his "Kitchen Cabinet," an informal group of trusted friends, supporters, kinsmen, and hangers-on, for advice and moral support. Van Buren did, however, enjoy a greater measure of influence in the administration than any previous vice president.

His last public statement, made the year before his death, was a declaration of his "earnest and vigorous support to the Lincoln Administration for...the maintenance of the Union and the Constitution" in response to President's Lincoln call for troops to suppress the rebellion. Lincoln reciprocated with a stilted posthumous tribute: "The grief of his patriotic friends, will measurably be assuaged by the consciousness that while...seeing his end approaching, his prayers were for the restoration of the authority of the government of which he had been head, and for peace and good will among his fellow citizens."

RICHARD MENTOR JOHNSON
9TH VICE PRESIDENT: 1837-1841

The United States Senate elected Richard Mentor Johnson of Kentucky the nation's ninth vice president on February 8, 1837. His selection marked the first and only time the Senate has exercised its prerogative under the U.S. Constitution's Twelfth Amendment, which provides, "if no person have a majority, then from the two highest numbers on the list, the Senate shall choose the Vice-President," Johnson became Martin Van Buren's running mate after three decades in the House and Senate, a congressional career spanning the administrations of five presidents from Thomas Jefferson through Andrew Jackson. Detractors alleged, however, that he owed his nomination solely to the dubious claim that he killed the Shawnee chieftain Tecumseh in 1813 at the Battle of the Thames. Throughout his career, Johnson professed allegiance to the principles of "Thomas Jefferson, the patriarch of republicanism," and correspondence from his early years in Congress suggests that he enjoyed a cordial acquaintance with Jefferson.

Johnson was on of the vociferous young congressmen, led by his fellow Kentuckian House Speaker Henry Clay, known collectively as the "war hawks." During the Twelfth Congress, this group urged military redress for

British violations of American frontiers and shipping rights,[58] and in June 1812 they voted to declare war against Great Britain. His nationalist perspective heightened by the war, Johnson joined with Henry Clay to advocating protection for frontier products and federal funding for internal improvements to give western producers readier access to eastern markets.

A legislative accomplishment that brought Johnson national distinction was a report that he prepared during his final Senate term, as chairman of the Committee on Post Offices and Post Roads, in response to a flood of petitions from religious congregations in the East demanding the suspension of Sunday mail deliveries. The January 19, 1829, report, widely reprinted in the press, argued that, as "a civil, and not a religious institution," the government could take no action sanctioning the religious convictions or practices of any denomination. After leaving the Senate, Johnson continued his crusade as a member of the House of Representatives. In 1830, as chairman of the House Committee on Post Offices and Post Roads, he submitted a second report. This, like the earlier Senate report, brought him widespread acclaim in the labor press as a champion of religious liberty.

Johnson was reelected to a full Senate term in 1822 but in 1828 lost his reelection bid because Kentucky Democrats feared that controversy over his domestic life would jeopardize Jackson's chances in the national election. Johnson never married. Family tradition recounts that he ended an early romance, vowing revenge for his mother's interference, after Jemima Johnson pronounced his intended bride unworthy of the family.[59] He later lived openly with Julia Chinn, a mulatto slave raised by his mother and inherited from his father, until her death from cholera in 1833. Johnson freely acknowledged the relationship, as well as the two daughters born to the union.

JOHN TYLER 10ᵀᴴ VICE PRESIDENT: 1841

He held the office of vice president for only thirty-three days; he presided over the Senate for less than two hours. Despite this brief experience, John Tyler significantly strengthened the office by enforcing an interpretation of the Constitution that many of his contemporaries disputed. Tyler believed that, in

---

[58] Marshall Smelser, *The Democratic Republic, 1801-1815* (New York, 1968), pp. 208-9; John Niven, John C. Calhoun and the Price of Union (Baton Rouge, LA, 1988), p. 36; Henry W. Fritz, "The War Hawks of 1812," *Capitol Studies 5* (Spring 1977): 28.

the event of a vacancy in the office of president, the vice president would become more than just the acting president. He would assume the chief executive's full powers, salary, and residence as if he himself had been elected to that position. Taken for granted today, that interpretation is owed entirely to this courtly and uncompromising Virginian who brought to the vice-presidency a greater diversity of governmental experience than any of his predecessors.

In the 1830s John Tyler identified himself with the Democratic Party but differed often with President Andrew Jackson. The two men diverged both in temperament – a Tidewater aristocrat opposing a Tennessee democrat – and in political philosophy. Tyler supported the president's veto of legislation re-chartering the Bank of the United States, but he opposed Jackson's removal of government funds from that institution.

Although Tyler at age fifty-one was younger than any previous president, he was also the most experienced in the ways of government. He had served as a member of both houses of his state legislature, both houses of the U.S. Congress, governor of his state, and vice president of the United States.[60] By appearance, he was cast for a leadership role. Standing slightly over six feet, he possessed all the "features of the best Grecian model" including a sharply defined aquiline nose. When a bust of Cicero was discovered during an excavation in Naples, two visiting Americans reportedly exclaimed "President Tyler!"[61]

The first vice president to succeed to the presidency upon the death of his predecessor, William Henry Harrison's demise after only a month in office presented the nation with a potential constitutional crisis. The Constitution of that time contained no Twenty-Fifth Amendment to lay out procedures governing the vice president's actions when the chief executive became disabled or when there was a vacancy before the end of the incumbent's term. The document provided only that the "Powers and Duties of the said Office...shall devolve on the Vice President...[who] shall act accordingly, until the Disability be removed, or a President shall be elected."

As the epithet "His Accidency" grew in popularity, Congress convened on May 31, 1841, for its previously called special session and immediately took up the issue of Tyler's claim to be president in his own right.

---

[59] Meyer, pp. 318-19.
[60] Seager, p. 147.
[61] Quoted in Remini, p. 582.

Despite his earlier ambitions, Tyler became the first president not to seek a second term. (No party would have him as its candidate.) Tyler biographer Robert Seager notes that he "lived in a time in which many brilliant and forceful men strode the American stage...and he was overshadowed by all of them, as was the office of the Presidency itself...Had he surrendered his states' rights and anti-Bank principles he might have salvaged it. He chose not to surrender and the powerful Henry Clay crushed him."[62]

GEORGE MIFFLIN DALLAS
11TH VICE PRESIDENT: 1845-1849

George Mifflin Dallas admitted in his later years that his driving force in life was for historical fame. From the 1840s on through the latter part of the nineteenth century, Americans associated his name with the acquisition of Texas and the settlement of the Oregon boundary dispute. Texas memorialized his contributions to the state's history by renaming the town of Peter's Corner in his honor. In the 1850s, when officials in Oregon sought a name for the principal town in Polk County, they settled on the logical choice: Polk's vice president. Thus, while largely forgotten today as the nation's eleventh vice president, George Mifflin Dallas has won his measure of immortality in a large Texas city and a small Oregon town.[63]

For four years at the heart of the Senate's "Golden Age," Vice President George Dallas occupied a center stage seat in the nation's premier political theater. This courtly Philadelphia aristocrat – whose political ambition greatly exceeded his political energy – entered that arena in 1845 filled with optimism for the nation, the Democratic Party, and his own presidential future. He departed in 1849 embittered and depressed, his political chances obliterated. During his term, the nation fought and won a war with Mexico, acquired vast new territories, settled a chronic northwestern boundary dispute, discovered gold, and launched a communications revolution with the invention of the telegraph. In the Senate, where political party caucuses assumed new powers to appoint committee members and distribute patronage, the central debates occurred over the status of slavery in the territories and the very nature of the constitutional union. With increasing frequency, senators faced conflicting

---

[62] Ibid., p. xvi.
[63] Lewis A. McArthur, *Oregon Geographic Names*, 5th ed. (Portland, OR, 1982), p. 205.

choices between the desires of their parties and of their constituencies. When such an unavoidable decision confronted Vice President Dallas in July 1846 on the then searing issue of tariff policy, he chose party over constituency – thereby forfeiting his political future.

Like many of his contemporaries on the national political stage in 1845, George Dallas wonted to be president. In accepting the Democratic nomination, Polk committed himself to serving only one term, hoping this promise would encourage his party's warring factions to suspend their combat at least until the 1848 campaign.[64] Instead, his pledge instantly prompted maneuvering from many quarters for the 1848 nomination. Four of the nation's previous vice presidents had moved up to the presidency and Dallas saw no reason why he should not become the fifth. For his first two years in the second office, Dallas framed his behavior with that goal in mind.

Dallas determined that he would use his vice-presidential position to advance two of the administration's major objectives: tariff reduction and territorial expansion. Dallas sought to avoid having to exercise his singular constitutional prerogative on the tariff issue, actively lobbying, Senators during the debate over Treasury Secretary Walker's tariff bill in the summer of 1846. Despite Dallas' efforts to avoid taking a stand, the Senate completed its voting on the Walker Tariff with a 27-to-27 tie. When he cast the tie-breaking vote in favor of the tariff on July 28, 1846, Dallas rationalized that he had studied the distribution of Senate support and concluded that backing for the measure came from all regions of the country. While Dallas' tariff vote destroyed him in Pennsylvania, his aggressive views on Oregon and the Mexican War crippled his campaign efforts elsewhere in the nation.[65] In his last hope of building the necessary national support to gain the White House, the vice president shifted his attention to the aggressive, expansionist foreign policy program embodied in the concept of "Manifest Destiny." He actively supported efforts to gain control of Texas, the Southwest, Cuba, and disputed portions of the Oregon territory.

The joint United States-British occupation of the vast western territory in the region north of the forty-second parallel and south of the boundary at fifty-four degrees, forty minutes, was scheduled for renewal in 1847. Dallas seized the opportunity in 1846 to call for a "settlement" at the 54° 40' line, even at the risk of war with Great Britain. For several months early in 1846, the vice

---

[64] Paul H. Beregeron, *The Presidency of James K. Polk* (Lawrence, KS, 1987), pp. 16-17.

president pursued this position – seeking to broaden his national political base – until President Polk and British leaders agreed to compromise on a northern boundary at the forty-ninth parallel. This outcome satisfied Dallas, as it removed his earlier fear that the United States would be caught in a two-front war, with Great Britain over the Oregon boundary and with Mexico over control of Texas. Now the nation would be free to concentrate on war with Mexico, a conflict that Dallas hoped would serve to unify the Democratic Party and propel him to the White House. As the Mexican War continued into 1846, Dallas expanded his own objective to the taking of all Mexico. Again, a moderate course advanced by more realistic leaders prevailed and forced Dallas to applaud publicly the result that gained for the United States the Mexican states of California and New Mexico. The events of 1846 extinguished Dallas' presidential fire.

MILLARD FILLMORE 12TH VICE PRESIDENT: 1849-1850

The new vice president needed a clerk. Millard Fillmore suffered from an eye disorder that limited his ability to read by candlelight, yet his official duties kept him so busy during the daytime that he had to put off reading and preparing his correspondence until evening. A clerk would be most useful. When Fillmore's immediate predecessor, George Dallas, took office in 1845, no funding was provided for a vice-presidential clerk because there had been no vice president since 1841, when John Tyler had succeeded to the presidency after the death of William Henry Harrison. Senator Willie Mangum (W-NC), who had fulfilled the office's major constitutional function as Senate president pro tempore from 1842 to 1845, had considered his duties too light to justify continuing the perquisite that Vice President Richard M. Johnson had enjoyed during his 1837-1841 term. Aware of these precedents, Fillmore asked Mangum, one of the Whig party's senior senators, to introduce the necessary authorizing resolution. When Mangum did so, a Democratic senator immediately objected, noting that former Vice President Dallas had gotten along just fine without a clerk. Mangum responded by citing the example of Vice President Johnson, also a Democrat. The Democratic senator withdrew his objection and Fillmore got his clerk. From this experience,

---

[65] Belohlavek, p. 118.

Fillmore may have learned both how much the Senate valued precedent and how little some of its members regarded the office of vice president.[66]

Millard Fillmore rose to the vice-presidency, in part, because he was from New York. In presidential elections from 1812 to 1968, that state had the nation's largest congressional delegation and therefore was entitled to cast more votes in the Electoral College than any other state. New York's electoral riches account for the fact that, during the century from 1801 to 1901, eight of the twenty-two vice presidents called that state home. In designing a presidential ticket that would attract large blocks of electoral votes, the national parties always paid very careful attention to New York political leaders.

Millard Fillmore would occupy the nation's second highest office for fewer than seventeen months. During his brief tenure, he suffered the fate of other vice presidents: his president ignored him, his state's party leaders undercut him, and the Senate over which he presided barely tolerated him. Yet the office benefited him, just as he improved it. The experience ratified and extended his stature as a significant national figure. When Zachary Taylor's death thrust Fillmore into the presidency, few seriously doubted that he was up to the job. His close relations with senators at a time when the Senate served as the final arbiter of crucial national policy issues eased passage of the vital compromise legislation that staved off national political disintegration for another decade. To his role as the Senate's president, Fillmore brought a deep knowledge and understanding of the institution's rules, precedents, and culture. Aware that the incendiary climate in the Senate chamber during 1850 could foster an explosion of devastating national consequence, he insisted on order, decorum, and fair play. For his successors, he provided a valuable example, couched in the spirit of Thomas Jefferson a half century earlier.

When the Whigs gathered at Philadelphia in June 1848, party leaders expected that General Taylor would win their presidential nomination. The Taylor-Fillmore ticket won New York State by a narrow margin, providing barely enough electoral votes to swing the election to the Whigs.

Millard Fillmore shared Zachary Taylor's belief in a strong legislature and a compliant executive. In a letter written immediately after his election, he explained that in all areas not directly covered by the Constitution, "as to all other questions of mere policy, where Congress has the constitutional right to

---

[66] U.S. Congress, Senate, *Congressional Globe*, 33d Cong., 1st sess., pp. 4-5.

legislate, the will of the people, as expressed through their representatives in Congress, is to control, and that will is not to be defeated by the arbitrary interposition of the [executive] veto power." By adhering to this classic Whig doctrine, Taylor and Fillmore hoped to avoid the toiling sectional controversies that could easily wreck their administration, leaving them to the people's representatives in Congress.

The death of John C. Calhoun on March 31 removed a tenacious opponent of the compromise Fillmore presided at the statesman's funeral in the Senate chamber on April 2. On the following day, responding to the deeply unsettled atmosphere, the vice president took an extraordinary step for a presiding officer – he addressed the Senate. His topic: the vice president's "powers and duties to preserve order."[67] Speaking in a solemn manner, Fillmore stated that when he had first entered the office, he had assumed he would not be called on to maintain order in a body with such a strong reputation for courtesy and deference. He soon realized that he had been naïve. To arm himself against the challenge of recurring disorderly behavior, he had consulted old Senate records and manuals of parliamentary practice for guidance.

On the following day, agreeing to Foote's interrupted proposal, the Senate appointed the Select Committee of Thirteen to prepare a suitable compromise measure. The committee reported on May 8, but for the remainder of the spring and into the summer the Senate heatedly debated the slavery-related issues that underlay the Benton-Foote controversy. Vice President Fillmore's estrangement from the Taylor administration deepened during this period and he turned his creative energies to service on the newly established Smithsonian Institution's board of regents.

On Saturday, April 17, 1850, the Senate resumed its consideration of the volatile legislation related to slavery issue and California statehood. Mississippi's senior senator, Henry S. Foote, made a motion to refer the various proposals to a special thirteen-member committee, which would reshape them into a new legislative plan. Since Missouri's Thomas Hart Benton favored compromise but disliked Henry Clay's specific plan, he offered an amendment to undercut Foote's motion. Seated in his accustomed

---

[67] *Congressional Globe*, 31st Cong., 1st sess., pp. 631-32. Out of his concern for proper decorum, Fillmore reportedly ordered the removal of the large urn of snuff that had traditionally been placed on the vice president's desk. He acted because its availability caused members to congregate there, talking loudly and obscuring his view of the chamber. (This story is drawn from the recollections of Senate Assistant Doorkeeper Isaac Bassett as reported in the *New York Times*, June 7, 1894.)

place at the dais, Vice President Fillmore ruled that Benton's motion was in order, citing as his authority Thomas Jefferson's *Manual of Parliamentary Practice.*

Anticipating his return to a happy life in Buffalo, Fillmore left a chilled White House on a bitterly cold March 4, 1853 and resumed his role as Buffalo's leading educator and philanthropist.[68] He served as the first chancellor of the University of Buffalo and the first president of the Buffalo Historical Society.

WILLIAM RUFUS DEVANE KING 13TH VICE PRESIDENT: 1853

On April 18, 1853, death cheated William King of his life's calling. Experience and temperament had uniquely prepared him to be the Senate's constitutional presiding officer, but tuberculosis denied him that role as vice president.[69] Between 1836 and 1850, King had won a record-breaking eleven elections to the post of Senate president pro tempore. At the time of his 1852 election to the vice-presidency, only one other member in the body's entire history had exceeded King's twenty-eight years and ten months of Senate

---

[68] Rayback, p. 416.

[69] On taking office as president pro tempore in January 1837, King offered the following observations about the Senate and the role of its presiding officer. They are similar in tone and formulation to those that Vice President Aaron Burr uttered on March 2, 1805.

"The Senate of the United States, gentlemen, if, from its very organization, the great conservative body in this republic. Here is the strong citadel of liberty. To this body the intelligent and the virtuous, throughout our widespread country, look with confidence for an unwavering and unflinching resistance to the encroachments of power on the one hand, and the effervescence of popular excitement on the other. Unawed and unseduced, it should firmly maintain the constitution of its purity, and present an impregnable barrier against every attack on that sacred instrument, come it from what quarter it may. The demon of faction should find no abiding place in this chamber, but every heart and every head should be wholly occupied in advancing the general welfare, and preserving, unimpaired, the national honor. To insure success, gentlemen, in the discharge of our high duties, we must command the confidence and receive the support of the people. Calm deliberation, courtesy toward each other, inspire that confidence and command that support. It becomes my duty, gentlemen, to banish (if practicable) from this hall all personal altercation; to check, at once, every remark of a character personally offensive; to preserve order, and promote harmony...I earnestly solicit your cooperation, gentlemen, in aiding my efforts promptly to put down every species of disorder." (U.S. Congress, Senate, *Register of Debates in Congress*, 24th Cong., 2d sess., pp. 618-19.)

service.[70] Warm-hearted and even-tempered, King personified balance and fairness in deeply disputatious times. Elected to the vice-presidential term that ran from March 4, 1853 to March 3, 1857, King was positioned to occupy center stage during such tumultuous future performances as the party rending 1854 struggle over the Kansas-Nebraska Act and – the single most dramatic act in the Senate's history – the 1856 caning of Massachusetts Senator Charles Sumner by a South Carolina representative. One can now only speculate about the calming role that this natural mediator might have played in such events, although, ultimately, personalities and minds much stronger than his would direct the fateful course to national disunion and civil war.

William King was far from a genius and he had little talent as an orator. These qualities were so well noted, during his lifetime that a fellow southerner, Senator Robert M. T. Hunter of Virginia, felt free to remark on them even in the speak-no-evil context of a funeral oration. Hunter was quick to acknowledge, however, that this guileless and self0effacing man was an individual of integrity, sound judgment, and rich experience, who could be stern "when the public interests or his personal honor required it." Hunter and others lamented the demise of such a moderate and conciliatory statesman at "a period like this [April 1853], pregnant with change, and teeming, perhaps, with great and strange events."[71] Symbolic of the sectional balance that King tried to achieve, the Virginia senator's eulogy was followed by one from a longtime friend from Massachusetts, the renowned orator Edward Everett.

---

[70] As early as 1824, King regularly served as the chairman of the Committee of the Whole, a long-since-abandoned parliamentary form by which a full Senate could expedite its proceedings. (John Milton Martin, "William Rufus King: Southern Moderate," Ph.D. dissertation, University of North Carolina, 1955, p. 81). Prior to 1890, the Senate elected its president pro tempore only when the vice president was away from the chamber. Election to that post during the Senate's first century was generally considered an acknowledgment of the Senate's respect for the individual's judicious temperament. In later years, the Senate designated a permanent president pro tempore for each Congress, usually the senior member of the majority party. (U.S. Congress, Senate, *The Senate, 1789-1989: Addresses on the History of the United States Senate*, by Robert C. Byrd, S. Doc. 100-20, 100th Cong., 1st sess., vol. 2, 1991, Chapter 6, vol. 4, *Historical Statistics*, 1993, pp. 647-53.)

[71] U.S. Congress, Senate, Congressional Globe, 33d Cong., 1st sess., pp. 19-21. See also U.S. Congress, *Obituary Address of the Death of the Hon. William R. King, of Alabama, Vice President of the United States, Delivered in the Senate and House of Representative of the United States, Eighth of December, 1853* (Washington, 1854), pp. 8-13, 37. Representative Sampson Harris (D-AL) also commented that King lacked "many of those great attributes of mind, which dazzle and lead captive the admiring throng..." (p. 37) and the *National Intelligence* began its obituary, "Not endowed with shining talents, though of excellent sense..." (April 20, 1853.)

Everett reminded all that when the Senate over the past several decades had needed a presiding officer in the absence of the vice president, its members "turned spontaneously" to Senator King. "He possessed, in an eminent degree, that quickness of perception, that promptness of decision, that familiarity with the now complicated rules of congressional proceedings, and that urbanity of manner, which are required in a presiding officer."[72]

As the regional positions hardened in the tumultuous early months of 1850, King lamented the "baneful spirit of party" that in dividing the South encouraged northern extremists. In April, King's seniority and moderate views earned him a place as one of two southern Democratic representatives on the Senate's Select Committee of Thirteen, appointed to review Henry Clay's compromise resolutions regarding territories and slavery. With a majority of the committee's members, he agreed that slavery was a "rightful" subject for legislative attention, but only in the legislatures of states and not of territories. Thus, King took the view of southern conservatives that the Constitution protected owners in their control of slave property until a territory became a state.[73] At home, he met bitter opposition from a faction of "Southern Rights" secessionists who argued that his voting record better reflected the interests of Massachusetts, but an equally large group of supporters praised his support for compromise, union, and peace. He counseled patience, optimistically expecting the North to respect southern rights, but warning that if section's actions jeopardized those rights – both constitutional and material – all southern men should "hurl defiance at the fanatical crew, and unitedly determine to defend their rights at every hazard and every sacrifice."

King's long quest for the vice-presidency had resumed immediately after he returned from France in 1846. However, his failure that year to regain his Senate seat, coupled with deep ideological divisions within the Alabama Democratic Party, denied him the support necessary to launch a vigorous national campaign. At the 1848 national convention in Baltimore, following the nomination of Michigan's Lewis Cass for the presidency, King's was among a half-dozen names placed before the delegates. On the first ballot, he came in third. On the second ballot, the convention selected Kentucky's General William O. Butler, a veteran of the War of 1812 and the Mexican War.[74]

---

[72] *Congressional Globe*, 33d Cong., 1st sess., p. 20.
[73] Remini, *Henry Clay: Statesman for the Union*, pp. 746-47.
[74] Martin, "William R. King and the Vice Presidency," pp. 46-49.

In January 1852, the Alabama state Democratic convention endorsed the Compromise of 1850 and directed the state's national convention delegates to support King for either the presidency or vice-presidency. At the jam-packed, tumultuous Baltimore convention, delegates selected Franklin Pierce on the forty-ninth ballot. In a peace gesture to the Buchanan wing of the party, Pierce's supporters allowed Buchanan's allies to fill the second position, knowing that they would select King. During the ensuing campaign, King's tuberculosis, which he believed he had contracted while in Paris, denied him the active behind-the-scenes role that he might otherwise have played.

March 24, 1853 near Matanzas, a seaport town sixty miles east of Havana, the gravely ill statesman, too feeble to stand unaided, became the nation's thirteenth vice president. Deciding that he would make every effort to return to the United States, King set sail for Mobile on April 6. He reached his Alabama plantation on April 17, but his struggle was at an end. The sixty-seven-year-old King died there the following day. An opposition newspaper praised his "purity and patriotism" and concluded, "[t]hough not, perhaps, brilliant, he was better – sensible, honest, never running into ultraism, but in the contests between the State and the federal government, maintaining the true conservative medium, so necessary to the preservation of the constitution, the rights of the States and the Republic."

JOHN CABELL BRECKINRIDGE
14TH VICE PRESIDENT: 1847-1861

The only vice president ever to take up arms against the government of the United States, John Cabell Breckenridge completed four years as vice president under James Buchanan, ran for president as the Southern Democratic candidate in 1860, and then returned to the Senate to lead the remnants of the Democratic Party for the first congressional session during the Civil War. Although his cousin Mary Todd Lincoln resided in the White House and his home state of Kentucky remained in the Union, Breckinridge chose to volunteer his services to the Confederate army. The United States Senate formally expelled him as a traitor. When the confederates were defeated, Breckinridge's personal secession forced him into exile abroad, bringing his promising political career to a bitter end.

When the Mexican War began, Breckinridge volunteered to serve as an officer in a Kentucky infantry regiment. In Mexico, Major Breckinridge won the support of his troops for his acts of kindness, being known to give up his horse to sick and footsore soldiers. After six months in Mexico City, he returned to Kentucky and to an almost inevitable political career. In 1849, while still only twenty-eight years old, he won a seat in the state house of representatives. In that election, as in all his campaigns, he demonstrated both an exceptional ability as a stump speaker and a politician's memory for names and faces. Shortly after the election, he met for the first time the Illinois legislator who had married his cousin Mary Todd. Abraham Lincoln, while visiting his wife's family in Lexington, paid courtesy calls on the city's lawyers. Lincoln and Breckinridge became friends, despite their differences in party and ideology. Breckinridge was a Jacksonian Democrat in a state that Senator Henry Clay had made a Whig bastion. In 1851, Breckinridge shocked the Whig party by winning the congressional race in Clay's home district, a victory that also brought him to the attention of national Democratic leaders. He arrived in Congress shortly after the passage of Clay's Compromise of 1850, which had sought to settle the issue of slavery in the territories. Breckinridge became a spokesman for the pro-slavery Democrats, arguing that the federal government had no right to interfere with slavery anywhere, either in the District of Columbia or in any of the territories.

In Congress, Breckinridge became an ally of Illinois Senator Stephen A. Douglas. When Douglas introduced the Kansas-Nebraska Act of 1854, which repealed the Missouri Compromise and left the issue of slavery in the territories to the settlers themselves – a policy known as "popular sovereignty" – Breckinridge worked hard to enact the legislation. Breckinridge supported the Kansas-Nebraska Act in the hope that it would take slavery in the territories out of national politics, but the act had entirely the opposite effect. Public outrage throughout the North caused the Whig party to collapse and new anti-slavery parties, the Republican and the American (Know-Nothing) parties, to rise in its wake.

Breckinridge was thirty-six years old – just a year over the constitutional minimum age for holding the office – and his election would make him the youngest vice president in American history.

As vice president in such a turbulent era, Breckinridge won respect for presiding gracefully and impartially over the Senate. The expansion of the nation forced them to move to a new, more spacious chamber. During those years, he observed, the Constitution had "survived peace and war, prosperity and adversity" to protect "the larger personal freedom compatible with public order."

Breckenridge counseled against secession. Early in 1859 a New York Times correspondent in Washington wrote that "Vice President Breckinridge stands deservedly high in public estimation, and has the character of a man slow to form resolves, but unceasing and inexorable in their fulfillment." At a time when the Buchanan administration was falling "in prestige and political consequence, the star of the Vice President rises higher above the clouds."

On Christmas Day, 1868, departing President Andrew Johnson issued a blanket pardon for all Confederates. John C. Breckinridge returned to the United States in February 1869.

HANNIBAL HAMLIN 15TH VICE PRESIDENT: 1861-1865

The emotional issue of slavery demolished the American political system during the 1850s: the Whig party disintegrated; the Democrats divided; and the Free Soil and American (or Know-Nothing) parties flourished briefly and died. Emerging from the wreckage of the old system, the Republican Party, which ran its first presidential campaign in 1856, drew converts from all of these parties. Within the new party stood men who had spent years fighting each other under different political banners. In constructing a presidential ticket in 1860, therefore, Republicans needed candidates who would reflect their complex construction and reinforce their new unity. They picked a presidential candidate, Abraham Lincoln, who was not only a westerner but a Whig who claimed Henry Clay as his political role model. To balance Lincoln, Republicans chose as their vice-presidential candidate Hannibal Hamlin, an easterner who had spent the bulk of his political career as a Democrat and who had battled Henry Clay when they served together in the United States Senate. Despite their differences, Lincoln and Hamlin shared an opposition to the expansion of slavery into the western territories, without being abolitionists.[75]

Politically, from the 1830s to the 1850s, Maine was an entrenched Democratic state, and the politically ambitious Hamlin joined the Democratic Party. In 1835 he was elected to the state house of representatives. Described

---

[75] See William E. Gienapp, *The Origins of the Republican Party, 1852-1856* (New York, 1987).

as "tall, and gracious in figure, with black, piercing eyes, a skin almost olive-colored, hair smooth, thick and jetty, a manner always courteous and affable," he fit easily into legislative politics, became a popular member of the house, and was soon elected its speaker. His most notable legislative achievement was to lead the movement to abolish capital punishment in Maine.

The slavery issue split the Maine Democratic Party into two factions. Hamlin's antislavery faction won the name "Woolheads" from its opponents. The Woolheads in turn labeled their adversaries, who opposed the Wilmot Proviso, "Wildcats." In addition to the slavery issue, temperance also divided the two factions, with Hamlin's "Woolheads" supporting prohibition laws and the "Wildcats" opposing them.

As political turmoil reigned, Hamlin's attention was distracted by the illness of his wife Sarah Jane Hamlin. Both Hannibal and Sarah Hamlin loved Washington's social life of dances, receptions, card playing, and theater-going. But Sarah's health declined so severely in 1855 that for a while he considered resigning his Senate seat. Sarah Jane Hamlin died from tuberculosis in April 1856.

To some degree, Sarah's illness provided political cover for Hannibal Hamlin at a time when he was under intense pressure to abandon the Democrats in favor of the newly formed Republican Party. Republican leaders were anxious for the popular Hamlin to join their party to balance the radicals who threatened to gain control. As the 1860 election approached, some Maine Republicans viewed Hamlin as a possible favorite-son candidate, in case the frontrunner, New York Senator William Seward, should falter. When Lincoln upset Senator William Seward, the vice presidential nomination was offered first to the Seward camp. The disappointed Seward men put no one forward for the second spot. There was strong support among the delegates for Cassius M. Clay, the Kentucky abolitionist, but Republican Party leaders thought him too radical. By contrast, Hamlin seemed a more "natural" choice, more moderate, and a friend of Seward's in the Senate. Hamlin won the nomination on the second ballot.[76] The Lincoln-Hamlin victory triggered the secession of the southern states. When asked by a friend from Maine what the future would hold, the new vice president replied, "there's going to be a war, and a terrible one, just as surely as the sun will rise tomorrow."

---

[76] Hunt, pp. 114-18, 152; John Russell Young, *Men and Memories, Personal Reminiscences* (New York, 1901), pp. 48-50; Hans L. Trefousse, *Andrew Johnson: A Biography* (New York, 1989), p. 115.

Hamlin considered himself the most unimportant man in Washington, ignored equally by the administration and the senators. He called his job "a fifth wheel on a coach" and identified the vice president as "a contingent somebody."

Throughout the war, Hamlin identified more with frustrated congressional radicals than with the more cautious President Lincoln. Those around Lincoln concluded that the vice president was not in close sympathy with the president but "was known as one who passively rather than actively strengthened a powerful cabal of Republican leaders in their aggressive hostility to Lincoln and his general policy." Lincoln did not appear to hold this against Hamlin.

Despite Hamlin's grumbling about the powerlessness of the vice-presidency, he was willing to stand for reelection in 1864. Hamlin assumed that Lincoln supported his nomination, but the president – an entirely pragmatic politician – doubted that Hamlin would add much strength to the ticket in what was sure to be a difficult reelection campaign, with the survival of the nation at stake. "To be Vice President is clearly not to be anything more than a reflected greatness," Secretary of the Senate John W. Forney wrote to console Hamlin. "You know how it is with the Prince of Wales or the Heir Apparent. He is waiting for somebody to die, and that is all of it." Hamlin maintained a dignified silence but was vexed by his defeat.

A few weeks after Hamlin returned to Maine, on the morning of April 15, 1865, he encountered a group of sorrowful men on the street in Bengor, who informed that Lincoln had been assassinated. Hamlin boarded a steamer for Washington to attend the president's funeral. At the White House, he stood side by side with Andrew Johnson at Lincoln's casket, causing those who saw them to note the irony that Hamlin had within a matter of weeks missed the presidency. None could have realized how differently the nation's history might have developed if Lincoln had been succeeded by Hamlin, who favored a Radical Reconstruction of the South, rather than by Johnson, who opposed it.

ANDREW JOHNSON 16TH VICE PRESIDENT: 1865

Vice President-elect Andrew Johnson arrived in Washington ill from typhoid fever. The night before his March 4, 1865, inauguration, he fortified himself with whiskey at a party hosted by his old friend, Secretary of the Senate John W. Forney. The next morning, hung over and confronting cold, wet, and windy weather, Johnson proceeded to the Capitol office of Vice President Hannibal Hamlin, where he complained of feeling weak and asked for a tumbler of whiskey. Drinking it straight, he quickly consumed two more. Then, growing red in the face, Johnson entered the overcrowded and overheated Senate chamber. After Hamlin delivered a brief and stately valedictory, Johnson rose unsteadily to harangue the distinguished crowd about his humble origins and his triumph over the rebel aristocracy. In the shocked and silent audience, President Lincoln showed an expression of "unutterable sorrow," while Senator Charles Sumner covered his face with his hands. Former Vice President Hamlin tugged vainly at Johnson's coattails, trying to cut short his remarks. After Johnson finally quieted, took the oath of office, and kissed the Bible, he tried to swear in the new senators, but became so confused that he had to turn the job over to a Senate clerk.[77]

Without a doubt it had been the most inauspicious beginning to any vice-presidency. "The inauguration went off very well except that the Vice President Elect was too drunk to perform his duties & disgraced himself & the Senate by making a drunken foolish speech," Michigan Republican Senator Zachariah Chandler wrote home to his wife. "I was never so mortified in my life, had I been able to find a hole I would have dropped through it out of sight." Johnson presided over the Senate on March 6 but, still feeling unwell, he then went into seclusion at the home of an old friend in Silver Spring, Maryland. He returned to the Senate only on the last day of the special session, March 11. Rumors that had him on a drunken spree led some Radical Republicans to draft a resolution calling for Johnson's resignation. Others talked of impeachment. President Lincoln, however, assured callers that he still had confidence in Johnson, whom he had known for years, observing, "It has been a severe lesson for Andy, but I do not think he will do it again."[78]

In the spring of 1861, Johnson took the train from Washington back to Tennessee and was mobbed at several stops in Virginia. The senator had to pull a pistol to defend himself. Although Union sympathies were strong in the eastern mountains of Tennessee, where Johnson's hometown of Greenville was located, he found Confederate flags flying around the town. There were

---

[77] H. Draper Hunt, *Hannibal Hamlin of Maine: Lincoln's First Vice-President* (Syracuse, NY, 1969), pp. 196-98; Lloyd Paul Stryker, *Andrew Johnson: A Study in Courage* (New York, 1929), p. 167.

[78] Hans L. Trefousse, *Andrew Johnson: A Biography* (New York, 1989), pp. 188-91; John W. Forney, *Anecdotes of Public Men* (New York, 1873), 1:177.

enough Union sympathizers in Tennessee to defeat an effort to call a state convention to secede, but after the firing on Fort Sumter, sentiment in the state swung more heavily to the Confederates. To avoid arrest, Johnson left Tennessee and returned to the Senate. As the only southern senator to remain loyal to the Union after his state seceded, Johnson became a hero in the North. As a leader of the "War Democrats," he denounced "Peace Democrats" and defended President Lincoln's use of wartime executive power. "I say, Let the battle go on – it is Freedom's cause…Do not talk about Republicans now; do not talk about Democrats now; do not talk about Whigs or Americans now; talk about your Country and the Constitution and the Union."

Lincoln faced a difficult campaign for reelection in 1864, and he doubted that his vice president, Maine Republican Hannibal Hamlin, would add much to his ticket. Officially, the president maintained a hands-off attitude toward the choice of a vice president, but privately he sent emissaries to several War Democrats as potential candidates on a fusion ticket. General Benjamin F. Butler let the president know he had no interest in the second spot, but Johnson of Tennessee and Daniel S. Dickinson of New York both expressed eagerness to be considered. Secretary of State William Seward, who counted New York as his own political base, wanted no part of Dickinson in the cabinet and threw his weight behind Johnson. The fearless, tough-minded war governor of Tennessee captured the imagination of the delegates. As John W. Forney judged Johnson's wartime record: "His speeches were sound, his measures bold, his administration a fair success." Johnson won the nomination on the first ballot.[79]

Late in October 1864 he addressed a large rally of African Americans in Nashville. Johnson noted that, since Lincoln's emancipation proclamation had not covered territories like Tennessee that were already under Union control, he had issued his own proclamation freeing the slaves in Tennessee. He also asserted that society would be improved if the great plantations were divided into many small farms and sold to honest farmers. Looking out over the crowd and commenting on the storm of persecution through which his listeners had passed, he wished that a Moses might arise to "lead them safely to their promised land of freedom and happiness." "You are our Moses," shouted people in the crowd. "We want no Moses but you!" "Well then," replied Johnson, "humble and unworthy as I am, if no other better shall be found, I will indeed be your Moses, and lead you through the Red Sea of war and bondage, to a fairer future of liberty and peace."

During Johnson's six weeks as vice president, he faced greater danger than he knew. The assassination plot that would make Johnson president included him as a target. When John Wilkes Booth arrived at the Kirkwood House and learned that Atzerodt was gone, he lost hope that this weak man would have the nerve to carry out his assignment. If he could not have Johnson killed, Booth improvised a way of discrediting him. He asked for a blank card, which he filled out: "Don't wish to disturb you. Are you at home? J. Wilkes Booth." Booth assumed that Johnson would have a hard time explaining the card, since it suggested that the vice president was himself part of the conspiracy. Fortunately for Johnson, his secretary, William A. Browning, picked up the mail at the desk and assumed that the card was for him, since he had once met Booth after a performance.

A pounding at the door later that evening awakened Andrew Johnson. Rather than George Atzerodt with a pistol, the excited man at the door was former Wisconsin Governor Leonard Farwell, who had just come from Ford's Theater and who exclaimed, "Someone has shot and murdered the President." At dawn, Johnson, receiving word from Secretary of War Edwin Stanton that Lincoln was dying, insisted on going to the president's side. Flanked by Governor Farwell and the provost marshal, the vice president walked the few blocks to the Petersen house, just across from Ford's Theater, where Lincoln had been carried. Admitted to the bedroom where the cabinet and military leaders were gathered around the president's deathbed, Johnson stood with his hat in his hand looking down saying nothing. He then took Robert Lincoln's hand, whispered a few words to him, conversed with Stanton, and went to another parlor to pay his respects to Mary Todd. Somberly, he walked back to Kirkwood House. There, in his parlor, at ten o'clock that morning after Lincoln's death, Johnson took the oath of office from Chief Justice Salmon P. Chase.[80]

Showing a strange amalgam of political courage and "pigheaded" stubbornness, Andrew Johnson confounded both his supporters and his adversaries. By the end of May 1865, it became clear that, like Lincoln, he intended to pursue a more lenient course toward Reconstruction than the

---

[79] Hunt, pp. 178-89; Trefousse, *Andrew Johnson*, pp. 176-79; Stryker, pp. 121-23; Forney, 1:166-67, 2:48.

[80] See Jim Bishop, *The Day Lincoln Was Shot* (New York, 1955).

Radicals in Congress wanted. Members of Congress grumbled when Johnson handed pardons to former Confederate leaders, suspected that the plebeian president took pride in having former aristocrats petition him. Congress was further shocked when the new governments formed under Johnson's plan enacted "Black Codes" that sought to regulate and restrict the activities of the freedmen.

That fall, Johnson conducted a disastrous "swing around the circle," campaigning by train in favor of congressional candidates who supported his policies. Egged on by hecklers, he made intemperate remarks that further alienated the voters and resulted in the election of an even more hostile Congress. The new Congress seized the initiative on Reconstruction from the president – most notably with a constitutional amendment giving the freedman the right to vote – and passed legislation to limit his responses. Among these laws, the Tenure of Office Act prohibited the president from firing cabinet officers and other appointees without Senate approval. Johnson considered the act unconstitutional – as indeed the Supreme Court would later declare it – and in February 1868 he fired his secretary of war, Edwin Stanton, for insubordination.[81]

Although Johnson's term was coming to a close and he had little chance of nomination by any party, the House of Representatives voted to impeach the president. The New York Tribune's editor Horace Greeley thought this a foolhardy tactic. "Why hang a man who is bent on hanging himself?" The two-thirds impeachers failed by a single vote to achieve the two-thirds majority necessary to convict the president.

The only former U.S. president ever to return to serve in the Senate, Johnson saw his election as a vindication and came back to Washington in triumph. A reporter asked if he would use his new position to settle some old scores, to which Johnson replied, "I have no enemies to punish nor friends to reward."

---

[81] Donald A. Ritchie, *Press Gallery: Congress and the Washington Correspondents* (Cambridge, MA, 1991), pp. 79-90; Foner, pp. 261-71.

SCHUYLER COLFAX 17TH VICE PRESIDENT: 1869-1873

As amiable a man who never served in Congress, good-natured, kindly, cordial, and always diplomatic, Indiana's Schuyler Colfax won the nickname "Smiler" Colfax. Through two of the most tumultuous decades in American public life, Colfax glided smoothly from the Whig to Know-Nothing to Republican parties, mingling easily with both conservatives and radicals. He rose to become Speaker of the House and vice president and seemed poised to achieve his goal of the presidency. Along the way, there were those who doubted the sincerity behind the smile and suspected that for all his political dexterity, Colfax stood for nothing save his own advancement. Those close to President Abraham Lincoln later revealed that he considered Speaker Colfax an untrustworthy intriguer, and President Ulysses S. Grant seemed relieved when the Republican convention dumped Vice President Colfax from the ticket in 1872. Even the press, which counted the Indiana editor as a colleague and pumped him up to national prominence, eventually turned on Colfax and shredded his once admirable reputation until he disappeared into the forgotten recesses of American history.[82]

Colfax served as a delegate to the Whig convention of 1848 and to the convention that drafted a new constitution for Indiana in 18498. He led the opposition to a provision in the constitution that barred African Americans from settling in Indiana or those already in the state from purchasing land. Despite his efforts, this radical barrier stood until ruled unconstitutional as a consequence of the Thirteenth Amendment to the Constitution in 1865. In 1851, the Whigs chose Colfax to run for Congress. Antislavery Whigs like Colfax sought to build a new party that combined the antislavery elements among the Whigs, Democrats, and Free Soilers, a coalition that eventually emerged as the Republican Party.

When the Thirty-eighth Congress convened in December 1863, House Republicans — with their numbers considerably thinned — elected Schuyler Colfax Speaker, despite President Lincoln's preference for a Speaker less tied to the Radical faction of his party.[83] As Speaker of the House, Schuyler Colfax

---

[82] James G. Blaine, *Twenty Years of Congress: From Lincoln to Garfield* (Norwich, CT, 1884), 1:497-98; Neil MacNeil, *Forge of Democracy: The House of Representatives* (New York, 1963), p. 69; Allan G. Bogue, *The Congressman's Civil War* (New York, 1989), p. 117.

[83] Charles Edward Russell, *Blaine of Maine: His Life and Times* (New York, 1931), p. 237; Bogue, p. 116; David Herbert Donald, *Lincoln* (New York, 1995), pp. 468-69.

presided, in the words of the journalist Ben: Perley Poore, "in rather a slap-dash-knock-'em down auctioneer style, greatly in variance with the decorous dignity of his predecessors." He had studied and mastered the rules of the House, and both sides considered his rulings fair. Credited as being the most popular Speaker since Henry Clay, Colfax aspired to be as powerful as Clay.

Colfax's efforts at party harmony and a moderate course of Reconstruction were short lived. The President's plan to reconstruct the South showed little regard for the rights of the freedmen, and he vetoed such relatively moderate congressional efforts as the Freedmen's Bureau bill. His action drove moderate and radical Republicans into an alliance that brought about congressional Reconstruction of the South.

As the 1868 presidential election approached, Speaker Colfax believed the nomination of Ulysses S. Grant to be "resistless." Colfax stayed in Washington while the Republican convention met in Chicago. His good friend, William Orton, head of the Western Union Telegraph Company, arranged for Colfax to receive dispatches from the convention every ten minutes. On May 21 Colfax was in the Speaker's Lobby when he received Orton's telegram announcing his nomination. Cheers broke out, and the room quickly filled with congressmen wishing to offer congratulations. On the Senate side, Bluff Ben Wade received the news that he had been beaten and said, "Well, I guess it will be all right; he deserves it, and he will be a good presiding officer."

For years, Colfax had addressed Sunday schools and temperance revival meetings, quoting from the Bible and urging his listeners to a life of virtue. He won support from the religious magazines as a "Christian Statesman." One campaign biography praised his "spotless integrity" and declared, "So pure is his personal character that the venom of political enmity has never attempted to fix a stain upon it." Democrats, however, lambasted Colfax as a bigot for the anti-Catholicism of his Know-Nothing past. Republicans dismissed these charges as mud-slinging and organized Irish and German Grant and Colfax Clubs to court the Catholic and foreign-born vote. (Although it was not known at the time, U.S. Grant had also once joined the Know-Nothings and apparently shared their anti-Catholic prejudices.)[84]

In November 1868, Grant and Colfax were narrowly elected over the Democratic ticket headed by New York Governor Horatio Seymour. There was much surprise, when in September 1870, at age forty-seven, Colfax announced that he intended to retire at the end of his term. This was an old tactic for Colfax, who periodically before had announced his retirement and then changed his mind. Some believed he intended the announcement to further separate himself from the Grant administration and open the way for the presidential nomination in 1872. But the national press and Senator Henry Wilson took the announcement at face value, and before long the movement to replace him went further than Colfax has anticipated.

Colfax predictably changed his mind early in 1872 and acceded to the wishes of his friends that he stand for reelection on "the old ticket." President Grant may have questioned Colfax's intentions. In 1871 the president had sent his vice president an extraordinary letter, informing him the Secretary of State Hamilton Fish wished to retire and asking him "in plain English" to give up the vice-presidency for the State Department. Grant appeared to be removing Colfax as a potential rival. "In all my heart I hope you will say yes," he wrote, "though I confess the sacrifice you will be making." Colfax declined, and a year later when Senator Wilson challenged Colfax for re-nomination, the president chose to remain neutral in the contest.[85]

As a man in his forties, Colfax might well have continued his political career after the vice-presidency, except for his connection to the worst scandal in nineteenth-century U.S. political history. In September 1872, as the presidential campaign was getting underway, the *New York Sun* broke the four-year-old story about the Crédit Mobilier, a finance company created to underwrite construction of the transcontinental Union Pacific Railroad. Since the railroad depended on federal subsidies, the company had recruited Massachusetts Representative Oakes Ames to distribute stock among the key members of Congress who could help them the most. Some members had paid for the stock at a low value, others had put no money down at all but simply let the generous dividends pay for the stock.

On January 7, 1873, the House committee investigating the Crédit Mobilier scandal called the vice president to testify. Ames' notes indicated that Colfax had received an additional $1,200 in dividends. On the stand, Colfax swore flatly that he had never received a dividend check form Ames.

---

[84] Russell, p. 237; Richardson, p. 560; Tyler Anbinder, *Nativism and Slavery: The Northern Know Nothings and the Politics of the 1850s* (New York, 1992), pp. 271-74.

[85] George S. Sirgiovanni, "Dumping the Vice President: An Historical Overview and Analysis," *Presidential Studies Quarterly* 24 (Fall 1994): 769-71.

Without missing a beat, Colfax insisted that Ames himself must have signed and cashed the check. Then the committee produced evidence from Colfax's Washington bank that two days after the payment had been made, he had deposited $1,200 in cash – and the deposit slip was in Colfax's own handwriting. A resolution to impeach Colfax failed to pass by a mostly party-line vote, in part because just a few weeks remained in his term. The pious statesman had been exposed, and the public was unforgiving. Colfax left the vice-presidency in disgrace, becoming a symbol of the sordidness of Gilded Age politics. Later in 1873, when the failure of the transcontinental railroads to make their bond payments triggered a disastrous financial collapse on Wall Street, plunging the nation into a depression that lasted for the rest of the decade, one ruined investor muttered that it was "all Schuyler Colfax's fault, damn him."

Doggerel from a critical newspaper perhaps served as the epitaph for Schuyler Colfax's rise to national prominence and precipitous fall from grace:

A beautiful smiler came in our midst,
Too lively and fair to remain;
They stretched him on racks till the soul of Colfax
Flapped up into Heaven again,
May the fate of poor Schuyler warn men of a smiler,
Who dividends gets on the brain![86]

HENRY WILSON 18ᵀᴴ VICE PRESIDENT: 1873-1875

Long before public opinion polling, Vice President Henry Wilson earned recognition as a master of reading the public's mind. During his eighteen years in the United States Senate, Wilson traveled relentlessly through his home state of Massachusetts. A typical day would find him visiting shops and factories around Boston. Then he would board the night train to Springfield, where he would rouse some political friend at 2 a.m. and spend the rest of the night talking over current issues, departing at dawn to catch the early train to Northampton or Greenfield. "After a week or two spent in that way," his friend George F. Hoar observed, never giving his own opinion, talking as if he were all things to all men, seeming to hesitate and falter and be frightened, so

---

[86] Summers, *The Press Gang*, p. 154.

if you had met him and talked with him you would have said…that there was no more thought, nor more steadiness of purpose, or backbone in him than in an easterly cloud; but at length when the time came, and he had got ready, the easterly could seemed suddenly to have been charged with an electric fire and a swift and resistless bolt flashed out, and the righteous judgment of Massachusetts came from his lips.[87]

Such systematic sampling of public opinion enabled Wilson to represent the prevailing sentiments of his constituents and to make remarkably accurate political prognoses. This skill helped him build political alliances and parties and win elections. It also added an element of opportunities to Wilson's political maneuvering that brought him distrust, even from his political allies. Yet he did not simply follow the winds of public opinion whichever way they blew. Throughout his long political career, Wilson remained remarkably consistent in his support for all men and women regardless of their color or class.

Henry Wilson's life resembled a Dickens novel. Like Pip, David Copperfield, and Nicholas Nickleby, he overcame a childhood of hardship and privation through the strength of his character, his ambition, and occasional assistance from others. He was born Jeremiah Jones Colbath on February 16, 1812, in Farmington, New Hampshire. His shiftless and intemperate father named the child after a wealthy bachelor neighbor in vain hope of inheritance. The boy grew to hate the name, and when he came of age had it legally changed to Henry Wilson, inspired either by a biography of the Philadelphia schoolteacher Henry Wilson or by a portrait of the Rev. Henry Wilson in a volume on English clergymen. Just outside of Boston he settled in the town of Natick, where he learned shoemaking from a friend.

The ambitious young cobbler worked so hard that by 1836 his health required he get some rest. Gathering his savings, Wilson traveled to Washington, D.C., to see the federal government. His attention was caught instead by the sight of slaves laboring in the fields of Maryland and Virginia and of slave pens and auctions within view of the Capitol Building. He left Washington determined "to give all that I had…to the cause of emancipation of America," he said. Wilson committed himself to the antislavery movement and years later took pride in introducing the legislation in Congress.

---

[87] George F. Hoar, *Autobiography of Seventy Years* (New York, 1903), 1:218.

As a self-made mad, Henry Wilson felt contempt for aristocrats, whether Boston Brahmins or southern planters. "I for one don't want the endorsement of the 'best society' in Boston until I am dead," he once declared," – for it endorses everything that is dead." He reserved even greater contempt for aristocratic southerners who lived off the labor of their slaves, swearing that slavery must be ended. "Freedom and slavery are now arrayed against each other," he declared; "we must destroy slavery, or it will destroy liberty."

Sadly disappointed in 1853 at the defeat of a new state constitution for which he had labored long and hard, Wilson responded by secretly joining the Order of the Star Spangled Banner, also known as the American or Know-Nothing party – an anti-Catholic and anti-immigrant, nativist movement. Given the collapse of the established parties, the Know-Nothings flourished briefly, offering Wilson an unsavory opportunity to promote his personal ambitions. In 1854, he ran as the Republican candidate for governor, but his strange maneuvering during and after the campaign convinced many Republicans that Wilson had sold them out by throwing the gubernatorial election to the Know-Nothings in return for being elected a U.S. senator by the Know-Nothings in the Massachusetts legislature, with the aid of Free Soilers and Democrats. Although Wilson identified himself as a Republican, his first Senate election left a residue of distrust that he would spend the rest of his life trying to live down.[88]

Henry Wilson soon stood among the inner circle of Radical Republicans in Congress beside Charles Sumner, Benjamin Wade, Thaddeus Stevens, and Henry Winter Davis. He introduced bills that freed slaves in the District of Columbia, permitted African Americans to join the Union army, and provided equal pay to black and white soldiers. Wilson pressed President Lincoln to issue an emancipation proclamation and worried that the final product left many people still enslaved in the border-states.

He was deeply disappointed in Johnson's endorsement of a speedy return of the Confederate states to the Union without any protection for the newly freed slaves. When the Thirty-ninth Congress convened in December 1865, Wilson introduced the first civil rights initiative of the postwar Congress. His bill aimed at outlawing the Black Codes and other forms of racial

---

[88] Ibid., pp. 46-64; Ernest A. McKay, "Henry Wilson: Unprincipled Know Nothing," *Mid-America 46* (January 1964): 29-37; David Herbert Donald, *Charles Sumner and the Coming of the Civil War* (Chicago, 1960), p. 268; William E. Gianapp, *The Origins of the Republican Party, 1852-1856* (New York, 1987), pp. 135-36.

discrimination in the former Confederacy but, deemed too extreme by the non-Radical Republicans, it was defeated. Wilson also proposed that the Constitution be amended to prohibit any effort to limit the right to vote by race.[89]

Johnson's more lenient policies for Reconstruction and his veto of the Freedmen's Bureau bill and other congressional efforts to protect black southerners eventually drove moderate Republicans into an alliance with the Radicals. Over time, Wilson saw his objectives added to the Constitution as the Thirteenth, Fourteenth, and Fifteenth amendments. He supported the use of federal troops to enforce congressional Reconstruction, to permit freedmen to vote, and to establish Republican governments in the southern states.

Just as the presidential campaign got underway in September 1872, the *New York Sun* published news of the Crédit Mobilier scandal, offering evidence that key members of Congress had accepted railroad stock at little or no cost. On the list were the names of Grant's retiring vice president, Colfax, and his new running mate, Henry Wilson. Newspaper correspondent Henry Van Ness Boynton sent the *New York Times* a dispatch reporting that Senator Wilson had made a "full and absolute denial" that he had ever owned Crédit Mobilier stock. In truth, Wilson had purchased the stock in his wife's name but had later returned it. Although the committee cleared Wilson of any wrongdoing in taking the stock, it concluded that the information Wilson had given the *Times* had been "calculated to convey to the public an erroneous impressions."

The Crédit Mobilier scandal did not dissuade voters from reelecting Grant and making Henry Wilson vice president. Wilson helped the ticket by embarking on an ambitious speaking tour that took him some ten thousand miles to deliver ninety-six addresses, ruining his health in the process. In May 1873, the sixty-one-year-old Wilson suffered a stroke that caused him to lose control of his facial muscles and to speak thickly whenever fatigued.

In the spring of 1875, Vice President Wilson made a six-week tour of the South, raising suspicions that he intended to "advertise himself" for the presidential nomination the next year. He returned home optimistic about the chances that the Republicans could build political and economic ties to conservative southerners by appointing a southern ex-Whig to the cabinet and

---

[89] Earl M. Maltz, *Civil Rights, the Constitution, and Congress, 1863-1869* (Lawrence, KS, 1990), pp. 43, 148; Michael Les Benedict, *A Compromise of Principle: Congressional Republicans and Reconstruction, 1863-1869* (New York, 1974), p. 24.

by offering economic aid to southern business. Although Grant desired a third term, Wilson's friends felt sure that the vice president could win the presidential nomination and election.[90]

During the nineteenth century, many members of Congress lived in boardinghouses and hotels where the plumbing left much to be desired. To accommodate them, the Capitol provided luxurious bathing rooms in its basement for the House and Senate. There members could soak in large marble tubs, enjoy a massage, and have their hair cut and beards trimmed. On November 10, 1875, Wilson went down to soak in the tubs. Soon after leaving the bath, he was struck by paralysis and carried to a bed in his vice-presidential office, just off the Senate floor. Within a few days, he felt strong enough to receive visitors and seemed to be gaining strength. When he awoke in his Capitol office on November 22, he was informed that Senator Orris Ferry of Connecticut had died. Wilson lamented the passing of his generation, commenting, "that makes eighty-three dead with whom I have sat in the Senate." Shortly thereafter, he rolled over and quietly died, at age sixty-three.

WILLIAM ALMON WHEELER
19TH VICE PRESIDENT: 1877-1881

In the wake of the Grant-era scandals, both the Republican and Democratic parties searched for untarnished candidates as they approached the presidential election of 1876. Republicans passed over their party's bigger names, men who had been stained by various exposés in the press, and settled instead on a ticket of Ohio Governor Rutherford B. Hayes and New York Representative William A. Wheeler. Although neither man was very well known to the nation, both had reputations for scrupulous honesty and independence.

Among the stranger individuals to occupy the vice-presidency, William Almon Wheeler seems to have been scarred by his father's ill health, which left him neurotically obsesses with his own well-being. An excessively cautious politician – to the point of timidity – he straddled the various factions in his party, avoided all commitments, and advanced himself politically while covering himself with obscurity.

---

[90] Abbott, p. 255.

Wheeler was elected to serve in the U.S. House of Representatives from 1861 to 1863. Wheeler stayed aloof from the New York state political machine run by Senator Roscoe Conkling. In the House, Wheeler generally kept silent unless he was managing a bill, but then he always proved to be well prepared and highly effective.

In March 1875, the House endorsed the "Wheeler compromise," a plan which essentially undid federal Reconstruction of the state and held out hope for peace between the North and South a decade after the Civil War had ended. The North seemed relieved to escape the responsibilities of Reconstruction. Representative Wheeler observed that northerners had expected too much from the South and declared that it was time to admit the failure of efforts to promote peace with the sword. His compromise taught northern Republicans how to cut their losses.

On election night, it looked as if Tilden and Hendricks had defeated Hayes and Wheeler, especially after Democrats captured Wheeler's home state of New York. Republican newspapers conceded the election, but Zachariah Chandler, chairman of the Republican National Committee, saw hope in the southern electors and dispatched telegrams to party leaders in those southern states still under Reconstruction rule, alerting them that the election was still undecided. One of the disputed states was Louisiana, where only a year earlier Wheeler had found evidence that the state board of election had produced fraudulent returns.

After a specially created electoral commission awarded all of the disputed ballots to Hayes, a joint session of Congress still had to count the ballots, and there was talk of angry Democrats marching on Washington by the thousands to prevent this "steal" of the election. To avoid bloodshed, friends of both candidates met at the Wormley Hotel in Washington in late February 1877. There they agreed to a compromise that settled the election and ended Reconstruction. In return for Hayes' election, Republicans offered federal funds to build railroads through the ravaged South and otherwise restore the southern economy, promised to appoint a southerner to the cabinet, and – most important – pledged to remove all federal troops from the southern states.

The Hayes family – scorned by many Washington politicos for their old-fashioned manner and strict adherence to temperance – became a surrogate family to the lonely vice president, a sixty-year old widower with no children.

Wheeler also provided Hayes with advice about appointments, recommending that selections be made according to "personal character, recognized capacity and experience." He especially warned Hayes about the hostility that the Conkling machine exhibited toward the new administration.

Wheeler made it easy for his nation to forget that he existed. A more assertive man might have risen to lead the opposition to the Conkling machine, but Wheeler contented himself with sneering at Conkling rather than challenging him. The vice president urged President Hayes not to appear weak and yielding to Conkling. But when Hayes took on Conkling by removing his lieutenants Chester A. Arthur and Alonzo Cornell from their lucrative posts at the New York customhouse, Wheeler disapproved the action because he feared it might split the party. Wheeler even endorsed Cornell's candidacy for governor of New York.[91]

In March 1881, Wheeler turned over the vice-presidency to his successor, Conkling's confederate Chet Arthur. He died on June 4, 1887, in Malone, a forgotten man.[92]

CHESTER ALAN ARTHUR 20TH VICE PRESIDENT: 1881

Following the Civil War and Reconstruction, "boss rule," and "machine politics" flourished in the United States, and nowhere more intensely than in New York, the most populated state in the Union. The Tweed Ring ran the Democratic Party's Tammany Hall apparatus in New York, and an equally powerful machine operated within the state's Republican party. Throughout the 1870s, that party's "stalwart" faction, led by Senator Roscoe Conkling, dominated New York politics until it reached both its apex and nadir within the space of a few months in 1881. Although responsible for some of the most tawdry politics in American history, Conkling's machine also produced two vice presidents, Chester Alan Arthur and Levi P. Morton, one of whom – Arthur – became president of the United States under tragic circumstances and turned against the machine and its spoilsmen.

A spellbinding orator with a commanding presence, Senator Roscoe Conkling was the uncrowned leader of the Senate in an era before majority and minority leaders were formally designated. One woman newspaper

---

[91] Williams, ed., p. 302; Otten, pp. 209, 256, 263.
[92] Jordan, pp. 407-8; Otten, pp. 277-79.

correspondent described him as the most alluring politician of his time and "the Apollo of the Senate." New York's other senator, Thomas C. Platt, similarly considered Conkling one of the handsomest men he had ever met.

The selection of Chet Arthur for vice president did not pacify Conkling, whom James A. Garfield knew was a man "inspired more by his hates than his loves." Party reformers were chagrined at the choice of Chet Arthur, the recently deposed collector of the port of New York and a symbol of corrupt machine politics, as Garfield's running mate. Most Republican newspapers held the vice-presidential candidate in low esteem. One campaign biography devoted 533 pages to Garfield and only 21 pages – almost as an embarrassed aside – to Arthur. Enumerating his "good" qualities, the campaign tract observed that his face was "full, fat, and fair," that he did not talk with "offensive accents," that he dressed "in perfect good taste," and that he was "fairly corpulent as his pictures very well suggest."

Conkling had good reason for apprehension. On March 23, Vice President Arthur, while presiding over the Senate, received a list of presidential nominations. His eye fell on the name of New York state senator William H. Robertson for collector of the port of New York, which, as one reporter described it, represented "a square blow at Conkling." At the Republican caucus, Conkling delivered a long, eloquent, and bitter attack on the president for his breach of senatorial courtesy. President Garfield retaliated by withdrawing the nominations of five of Conkling's men.

Vice President Arthur had no trouble deciding which side to take in this epic struggle between his president and his party boss. J. L. Connery, the editor of the *New York Herald*, which the Conkling machine courted, recalled Arthur telling him in confidence that Garfield had been neither honorable nor truthful. "It is a hard thing to say of a President of the United States, but it is, unfortunately, only the truth," said Arthur.

On July 2, Platt withdrew from the race in a last-ditch attempt to improve Conkling's chances of reelection. That same day, on the brink of victory, President Garfield walked arm in arm with Secretary of State Blaine through Washington's Baltimore and Ohio railroad station. A crazed assassin shot the president in the back and then identified himself with Conkling's stalwarts. After lingering throughout the summer, the mortally wounded Garfield died on September 19. By then the New York legislature had rejected Conkling's bid for reelection. "How can I speak into a grave?" Conkling complained.

Garfield's death elevated to the presidency a man who had shared an apartment in Washington with Conkling and who had sided with Conkling against Garfield. Political observers naturally assumed that Conkling would dominate Chet Arthur's administration.

Since the martyred President Garfield was regarded as a "victim of that accursed greed for spoils of office," his death rallied public support behind civil service reform legislation. In Arthur's first annual message to Congress in December 1881, he pledged his willingness to enforce any reform legislation that Congress might enact modeled on the British civil service system. Democratic Senator George H. Pendleton of Ohio sponsored a measure that became known as the Pendleton Act, which President Arthur signed in January 1883. The Pendleton Act established a bipartisan Civil Service Commission to set rules by which federal jobs would be filled. As the journalist Henry Stoddard mused, it was a strange turn of events that a spoilsman like Chester Arthur should sign the first effective civil service law and also be the first president to veto a river and harbor appropriations bill as excessive " – the bill that had come to be known as the 'pork barrel' bill into which both parties dug deep."

Rapidly declining in health, he died on November 17, 1886, less than two years after leaving the White House. He had been chosen as vice president without much expectation but, when thrust into the presidency, he rose to the occasion and conducted the office with style.

THOMAS ANDREWS HENDRICKS 21ST VICE PRESIDENT: 1885

American political parties have traditionally been coalitions of contradictory and contentious forces. The Electoral College is largely responsible for the loose-knit nature of these political parties. Victory requires a majority of electors from throughout the nation, a feat nearly impossible for any party rooted in a single region or clustered about one ideology or interest group. To build such national coalitions, politicians must reach out to those with whom they may disagree. The Democratic Party emerged from Thomas Jefferson's defense of the yeoman farmer against Alexander Hamilton's efforts to use the government to promote American industry and finance. Yet to build a national party, Jefferson needed to embrace New York's Tammany Hall, which represented urban interests. Nearly a century later, Indiana's Thomas A. Hendricks confronted that same split. He was a "soft-money" agrarian reformer, who ran twice for vice president on Democratic tickets headed by two different "hard-money" New York governors.

Always ambitious, Thomas Andrews Hendricks plunged into politics. When the Civil War erupted in 1861, the Democratic Party in Indiana divided between peace and pro-Union factions. Jesse D. Bright, the president pro tempore of the U.S. Senate, led the party's peace wing, while Hendricks became the leading "War Democrat." The legislature elected Thomas Hendricks to take the seat during the next full term. Bright thereafter blamed Hendricks for his defeat.[93]

Hendricks took his oath as a U.S. senator in 1863, becoming one of only ten Democrats facing thirty-three Republicans. President Abraham Lincoln cultivated the support of War Democrats like Hendricks. As Congress prepared to adjourn in March 1865, Hendricks paid a last visit to the president, who told him, "We have differed in politics, Senator Hendricks, but you have uniformly treated my administration with fairness." During the period of congressional Reconstruction of the South that followed the war, Hendricks never missed an opportunity to remind Republican senators that President Lincoln had opposed such radical Reconstruction measures as the Wade-Davis bill and had wanted a speedy return of the southern states to the Union. Hendricks consistently opposed repealing the fugitive slave laws until slavery was constitutionally abolished, and he tried to prevent African Americans from getting the right to vote. "I say we are not of the same race," Hendricks declared; "we are so different that we ought not to compose one political community."

Hendricks attended the Democratic National Convention in 1884 not as a candidate but rather as a delegate who would nominate former Indiana Senator Joseph E. McDonald. His appearance at the convention drew much enthusiastic applause, since he represented the "old ticket" of 1876 that had been robbed of victory. As the convention moved toward nominating the reform governor of New York, Grover Cleveland, Cleveland's opponents – especially New York City's Tammany Hall – concluded that Hendricks was the only man around whom the opposition could be united. They planned a strategy to stampede the convention to Hendricks the next day. Just as Indiana swung its vote to him, Hendricks entered the convention hall through a door facing the delegates. The band struck up a tune as Tammany Hall boss John

---

[93] Holcombe and Skinner, pp. 195, 245.

Kelly and his henchmen leaped from their seats and began shouting for Hendricks. As the delegated paraded, Hendricks sat calmly. "To those near him," Indiana Senator Daniel Voorhees asserted, "he simply appeared to enjoy in quiet silent way the popular approval of his long and faithful services."

These tactics might have worked, except that Cleveland's managers got wind of the conspiracy and sent messages to all the delegates warning them not to get caught up in any spurious demonstrations. Cleveland's supporters argued that New York was essential for a Democratic victory and that Cleveland, a hard-money reform governor, could attract liberal Republican voters, a group known as mugwumps. These arguments prevailed, and the Hendricks boom fizzled when Illinois increased its vote for Cleveland, followed by enough other states to give Cleveland the nomination at the end of the second ballot. Hendricks was rewarded with the vice-presidential nomination, once again to balance a hard-money presidential candidate and to offer the promise of carrying the swing state of Indiana.[94]

The prospect of victory invigorated Hendricks, and he campaigned valiantly, proving "a tower of strength for the ticket" in what has often been described as the "dirtiest" campaign in American political history. He attacked the incumbent Republican administration, helped stop a party bolt by Tammany Hall, drew large crowds to his speeches, and dramatically survived a late-night train wreck while campaigning in Illinois. Hendricks won praise as an "urbane leader." He stood five feet nine inches tall and was described as "well proportioned and stoutly built, though not corpulent." His once light hair had turned silver, and he wore "the least of side whiskers, which are light gray, and his complexion is fair." As a speaker he was clear and forceful, while in conversation he was "easy, courteous, cautious, and deferential.[95]

In 1884, Democrats won their first presidential election since 1856. From the start, however, Hendricks found himself at odds with President Cleveland, a scrupulously honest man with good intentions but limited vision. Unlike Hendricks, who had long called for more government intervention in the economy to promote agrarian reform, Cleveland advocated laissez-faire economics and was a Social Darwinist who thought the slightest hint of government paternalism would undermine the national character.

---

[94] Eaton, p. 11; Nevins, p. 154n; Poore, p. 284; Richard E. Welch, Jr., *The Presidencies of Grover Cleveland* (Lawrence, KS, 1988), pp. 28-29.

[95] Nevins, p. 177; Hensel, p. 255; Holcombe and Skinner, pp. 7, 363-64.

In September, Hendricks left Washington to attend the thirty-fifth anniversary reunion of the surviving members of the constitutional convention of Indiana and to rest in anticipation of the coming session of Congress in December. While at home in Indianapolis, he died in his sleep on November 25, 1885.

Hendricks' death eliminated the leader of the possible rival camp to Cleveland's presidency, but also for the second time in a decade deprived the nation of a vice-president for more than three years, raising concerns about the problem of presidential succession. If Cleveland should die, who would become president? On the recommendation of Massachusetts Republican Senator George F. Hoar, Congress in 1886 adopted a law that eliminated congressional officers from the line of succession in favor of cabinet officers, in order of their rank. This system prevailed until 1947, when the death of a president had again left the vice-presidency open for almost an entire year, stimulating another re-evaluation and a different solution to the problem.[96]

When President Cleveland ran for reelection in 1888, Democrats had to choose a replacement for Thomas Hendricks. Although Cleveland won a plurality of the popular vote, he lost the Electoral College and with it the presidency.

LEVI PARSONS MORTON 22ND VICE PRESIDENT: 1889-1893

Like a hero from the pages of a Horatio Alger novel, Levi P. Morton worked his way up by pluck and luck to fame and fortune. From a boy toiling in a country store, he rose to become one of the nation's wealthiest and most influential bankers and vice president of the United States. Morton might have become president as well, had his political acumen matched his financial ability.

Morton's gracious manners and generous campaign contributions made him many friends in Washington, among them President Ulysses S. Grant and Grant's strongest supporter in Congress, Senator Roscoe Conkling of New York.

---

[96] Chester L. Barrows, *William M. Evarts, Lawyer, Diplomat, Statesman* (Chapel Hill, NC, 1941), p. 446; Richard E. Welch, Jr., *George Frisbie Hoar and the Half-Breed Republicans* (Cambridge, MA, 1971), p. 137; John D. Feerick, *From Failing Hands: The Story of Presidential Succession* (New York, 1965), pp. 140-46.

In politics, Morton identified himself with the New York political faction, the "stalwarts," Conkling. Opposing the stalwarts were the "half-breed" Republicans who rallied behind Senator James G. Blaine of Maine. Conkling and Blaine were bitter personal political rivals, yet few substantive differences existed between their rival factions on the issues of the day. Morton's presence in the Conkling machine attested to its connections with Wall Street financiers.

The newspaper reporter George Alfred Townsend described Morton as "not a loquacious man, and yet an interesting talker, and one of the pleasantest expression of his face if that of the respectful, intelligent listener." He stood six feet tall, straight-limbed and erect, and walked with "flexible and quiet movements." With close-cropped hair and a square jaw, his face had a cosmopolitan appearance, "though the New England lines are decided." The "whole tone of his talk and character are toward tranquility," Townsend observed. In the House, Morton was "a close listener, a silent critic, a genial answerer, neither intrusive nor obtrusive." Morton won a reputation for his urbanity and generous hospitality. Among the friends he made was Representative James Garfield of Ohio.

In 1880, Morton went to the Republican convention as a Conkling lieutenant, dedicated to winning a third-term nomination for Ulysses S. Grant. Once Garfield won the nomination, he realized that he would need a New Yorker on the ticket and immediately though to his wealthy and well-positioned friend, L. P. Morton. Morton scurried to find Conkling, who objected. When Morton declined the offer, the vice-presidential nomination went instead to another Conkling man, Chester A. Arthur, who had fewer scruples about breaking with the boss.

When James G. Blaine, declining in health, made it clear he would not run again for president in 1888, Tom Platt threw New York's support to Indiana Senator Benjamin William Henry Harrison. Blaine recommended Harrison as the best candidate and suggested for vice president former Representative William Walter Phelps of New Jersey. However, Platt's support of Morton helped the banker defeat Phelps by a margin of five to one. The ticket of Harrison and Morton put together a strange victory in the presidential election. They lost the popular vote by 90,000 but still managed to beat the incumbent President Grover Cleveland in the Electoral College, 233 to 168. The journalist Arthur Wallace Dunn attributed the Republican success in 1888 to the combined political shrewdness of Republican National Committee chairman and Pennsylvania Senator Matt Quay and New York party boss Tom Platt.[97]

A thoughtful man, Harrison was cold in person but articulate and compelling as a public speaker. By contrast, Vice President Morton was no public speaker, but "a loveable personality," who "filled every position with grace, dignity, and ability." In an era of greed, corruption, and excess, Harrison and Morton both epitomized family life and puritanical religious values. Harrison's cabinet was conservative and business oriented, with the department store magnate John Wanamaker serving as postmaster general.

Just as Harrison's cabinet was called the "businessman's cabinet" for its inclusion of Wanamaker and the Vermont marble baron Redfield Proctor, the Senate over which Vice President Morton presided was dubbed a "millionaires' club." In the late nineteenth century, businessmen had steadily gained control over both the Republican and Democratic parties and used their political positions to advance their economic interests.

President Harrison considered the greatest failure of his administration to be its inability to pass the federal elections bill sponsored by Henry Cabot Lodge. Known as the "Force bill," it was intended to force the South to permit black men to vote and thereby protect their civil rights. The elections bill reached the Senate floor only because of Vice President Morton's tie-breaking vote. But the bill immediately encountered another filibuster, and Morton did nothing to help Republican efforts to break it.

As the Republican convention approached in 1892, Morton's supporters floated his name for the presidency, but he lacked the necessary delegate votes.

Morton died on his ninety-sixth birthday in 1920, already a long-forgotten name in both banking and politics.

---

[97] Robert F. Wesser, "Election of 1888," in *History of American Presidential Elections, 1789-1968*, ed. Arthur M. Schlesinger, Jr., and Fred L. Israel (New York, 1969), 2:1635; Arthur Wallace Dunn, *From Harrison to Harding: A Personal Narrative, Covering a Third of a Century, 1888-1921* (Port Washington, NY, 1972; reprint of 1922 edition), 1:8.

ADLAI EWING STEVENSON
23RD VICE PRESIDENT: 1893-1897

In February 1900, the Chicago American ran a photograph of former Vice President Adlai Stevenson holding his new grandson, Adlai Ewing Stevenson II. That year the grandfather was again nominated to run for vice president on the Democratic ticket. A half-century later, the grandson would run twice as the Democratic nominee for president and gain even greater national and international prominence. Yet it was the grandfather who came closest to becoming president of the United States – when President Grover Cleveland underwent critical surgery.[98]

Stevenson served as a delegate to the Democratic convention of 1884 that nominated Grover Cleveland for president. Cleveland's reform record as governor of New York helped win over Republican reformers, the mugwumps, who enabled him to defeat the popular but scandal-ridden Republican candidate James. G. Blaine.

When First Assistant Postmaster General Malcolm Hay, a civil service reformer, resigned due to ill health after only three months in office, Cleveland appointed the more partisan Adlai Stevenson to succeed him. Given free rein to remove Republican officeholders, Stevenson thoroughly enjoyed swinging the axe. One Republican journalist described Stevenson as "an official axman who beheaded Republican officeholders with the precision and dispatch of the French guillotine in the days of the Revolution." Dubbed "the Headsman" for replacing some 40,000 Republicans with deserving Democrats, he once "decapitated sixty-five Republican postmasters in two minutes."

When Democrats chose Cleveland once again as their standard bearer in 1892, they appeased party regulars by the nomination of the "headsman of the post-office," Adlai Stevenson, for vice president. As a supporter of using greenbacks and free silver to inflate the currency and alleviate economic distress in the rural districts, Stevenson balanced the ticket headed by Cleveland, the hard-money, gold standard supporter.

Civil service reformers held out hope for the second Cleveland administration but saw Vice President Stevenson as a symbol of the spoils

---

[98] Jeff Broadwater, *Adlai Stevenson and American Politics: The Odyssey of a Cold War Liberal* (New York, 1994), p. 1.

system. Just before Cleveland took office, a financial panic on Wall Street had plunged the nation into depression. As a staunch advocate of limited government, Cleveland disapproved of any government program to reduce economic suffering. By contrast, Vice President Stevenson represented the "populist doctrines" of currency reform that were creeping into the Democratic Party. In June 1893, after Cleveland proposed repeal of the Sherman Silver Purchase Act and a return to the gold standard.

In October 1893, efforts to repeal the Sherman Silver Purchase Act met with a filibuster in the Senate. Indiana Senator Daniel Voorhees, leader of the Cleveland Democrats, announced that the Senate would remain in continuous session until a vote was taken. Opponents made repeated calls for quorums, feigned illness, and refused to appear even when summoned by the Senate sergeant at arms. Repeal of the Sherman Silver Purchase Act only contracted the currency and further weakened the economy.

Adlai Stevenson enjoyed his role as vice president, presiding over "the most august legislative assembly known to men." He won praise for ruling in a dignified, nonpartisan manner. In personal appearance he stood six feet tall and was "of fine personal bearing and uniformly courteous to all."

Stevenson was mentioned as a candidate to succeed Cleveland in 1896. Stevenson received a smattering of votes, but the convention was taken by storm by a thirty-six-year-old former representative from Nebraska, William Jennings Bryan, who delivered his fiery "Cross of Gold" speech in favor of a free-silver plank in the platform. Not only did the Democrats repudiate Cleveland by embracing free silver, but they also nominated Bryan for president. Many Cleveland Democrats, including most Democratic newspapers, refused to support Bryan, but Vice President Stevenson loyally endorsed the ticket. In the fall, Bryan conducted the nation's first whistle-stop campaign, traveling extensively around the country and capturing people's imagination. Although he did far better than expected, he lost the election to Ohio's Republican governor, William McKinley.[99]

The Populists had already nominated the ticket of Bryan and Charles A. Towne, a silver Republican from Minnesota, with the tacit understanding that Towne would step aside if the Democrats nominated someone else. Bryan preferred his good friend Towne, but Democrats wanted one of their own, and the regular element of the party felt comfortable with Stevenson. Towne

---

[99] Merrill, *William Freeman Vilas*, p. 198.

withdrew and campaigned for Bryan and Stevenson. As a result, Stevenson, who had run with Cleveland in 1892, now ran with his nemesis Bryan in 1900. Twenty-five years senior to Bryan, Stevenson added age and experience to the ticket. Nevertheless, their effort never stood a chance against the Republican ticket of McKinley and Theodore Roosevelt.

Adlai Stevenson died in Bloomington on June 14, 1914. Thirty-eight years later, his grandson and namesake, then serving as governor of Illinois, agonized over whether to make himself available for the Democratic nomination for president. When Adlai E. Stevenson II appeared on the television news show *Meet the Press*, a reporter from the *Chicago Daily News* pressed him for a commitment by saying: "Wouldn't your grandfather, Vice President Stevenson, twirl in his grave if he saw you running away from a chance to be the Democratic nominee in 1952?" Stevenson, who loathed giving up his governorship for what most likely would be a futile campaign against the war hero Dwight Eisenhower, blanched at the comparison and replied, "I think we have to leave Grandfather lie."[100]

GARRET AUGUSTUS HOBART
24TH VICE PRESIDENT: 1897-1899

It seems startling that someone who never held prior office outside of a state legislature could be nominated and elected Vice President of the United States, as was Garret Augustus Hobart in 1896. By the time convention delegates chose the last nineteenth-century vice president, they had come to regard that office as little more than a "fifth wheel to the executive coach." The nomination was in their view simply a device for balancing the ticket, either by ideology or by region. "Gus" Hobart, an easterner chosen to run with a middle westerner, William McKinley of Ohio, completely shared McKinley's conservative political philosophy. With warm feelings for Hobart, President McKinley decided to rescue the vice-presidency from its low estate. McKinley so embraced the vice president as his friend, associate, and

---

[100] McKeever, p. 185.

confidant that Hobart's home on Lafayette Square became known as the "Little Cream White House," and Hobart as the "Assistance President."[101]

A rotund, jovial, hospitable man, Hobart displayed much tact, charm, and ability to work with other people. These qualities, which made him an outstanding state legislator, should have helped him move up to the national legislature. Several times Hobart stood for the United States Senate but never fought hard enough to win election from a state legislature in which he was immensely popular. He served instead as chairman of the State Republican Committee from 1880 to 1891 and as a member of the party's national committee.[102]

In 1896, the New Jersey delegation went to the Republican convention in St. Louis determined to nominate Hobart for vice president. Hobart insisted that he had not sought the nomination but that it was handed to him as "a tribute from my friends." It came equally as a tribute from Marcus A. Hanna, the Cleveland industrialist and political strategist who masterminded McKinley's nomination. Hanna wanted a ticket to satisfy the business interests of America, and Hobart, a corporate lawyer, fit that requirement perfectly. Hanna's biographer noted that, even if Hobart did little to strengthen the ticket, "he did nothing to weaken it."[103] Hobart himself felt ambivalent about the honor. Ambitious for national office, he was realistic enough to know what it would ultimately cost him.

For a running mate, McKinley had preferred Speaker Thomas B. Reed, with whom he had worked for many years in the House, but Reed would accept only the top spot on the ticket. Although McKinley and Hobart were strangers by comparison, the president had no difficulty warming up to Gus Hobart. The wealthy Hobart leased a house at 21 Lafayette Square, which became known as the "Little Cream White House." Built in 1828 by Col. Ogle Tayloe, the house had hosted Washington's high society during the antebellum years.

No previous vice president had visited the White House as often as Gus Hobart, due in part to the warm friendship that developed between Ida

---

[101] David S. Barry, *Forty Years in Washington* (Boston, 1924), p. 246; David Magie, *Life of Garret Augustus Hobart, Twenty-fourth Vice President of the United States* (New York, 1910), p. 169.

[102] Magie, pp. 27-57; Edward S. Ellis, et al., *Great Leaders and National Issues of 1896* (William Ellis Scull, 1896), p. 542.

[103] Ibid., pp. 58, 74; Margaret Leech, *In The Days of McKinley* (New York, 1959), p. 83; Herbert D. Croly, *Marcus Alonzo Hanna* (New York, 1912), p. 191.

McKinley and Jennie Hobart. Mrs. McKinley suffered from epilepsy, which left her a recluse in the White House. President McKinley doted on his wife and grew to depend on Jennie Hobart, who visited Ida daily. "The President constantly turned to me to help her wherever I could," Mrs. Hobart wrote in her memoirs, " – not because I was Second Lady, but because I was their good friend."

Arthur Wallace Dunn, a newspaper correspondent who covered presidents from Benjamin Harrison to Warren Harding, marveled that "for the first time in my recollection, and the last for that matter, the Vice President was recognized as somebody, as a part of the Administration, and as a part of the body over which he presided." Dunn described Hobart as a "business politician," whose knowledge of the "relations between business and politics" made his judgments extremely useful. McKinley even turned to his vice president for personal financial advice. Having once suffered the embarrassment of declaring personal bankruptcy, McKinley turned over a portion of his monthly presidential salary, which Vice President Hobart invested for him.[104]

Although Hobart socialized more frequently and worked more closely with the president than had most of his predecessors, his primary function remained that of presiding over the Senate. Hobart settled comfortably into the job.

In 1898, following the unexplained sinking of the U.S. battleship *Maine* in Havana harbor, sentiment in the Senate swung sharply toward war with Spain, which at that time still ruled Cuba as a colony. President McKinley's cautious attempts to avoid going to war made him seem indecisive. Accepting the inevitable, McKinley called on Congress to declare that a state of war existed with Spain. Hobart sent the president a pen to sign the declaration.[105]

The "splendid little war" with Spain was fought and won within a six-month period. At the conclusion of the fifty-fifth Congress, Vice President Hobart congratulated the Senate on this remarkable achievement, noting that "unlike any other session in the history of our country, this Congress has witnessed the inception, prosecution, and conclusion of a war." More than just

---

[104] *Address of Honorable John W. Griggs*, p. 9; Arthur Wallace Dunn, *From Harrison to Harding: A Personal Narrative, Covering a Third of a Century, 1888-1921* (Port Washington, NY, 1972; reprint of 1922 edition), 1:224-25; Morgan, p. 321.

[105] Horace Samuel Merrill and Marion Galbraith Merrill, *The Republican Command, 1897-1913* (Lexington, KY, 1971), p. 49; Leech, pp. 184-85, 193; Hobart, pp. 58-60.

a war Congress, it had also been a peace Congress, having approved the ratification of the Treaty of Paris that ended the Spanish-American War.

The vice president played a significant part in one aspect of that peace treaty. Although the United States had pledged not to take Cuba as its own territory, it did decide to hold the Philippine Islands, unexpectedly acquired from Spain. After the Senate had approved the peace treaty by the necessary two-thirds vote, Georgia Democrat Augustus O. Bacon had sponsored an amendment promising independence to the Philippines if it established a stable government. Due to the absence of several administration supporters, the vote was tied at 29 to 29. Hobart assured the taking of the territory for the United States by casting the deciding vote against Bacon's amendment.[106]

Despite the senators' many differences, Hobart as presiding officer observed that each of them stood on the common ground of patriotism, pride in the nation's history, zealousness for its Constitution, and devotion to its flag. For a generation old enough to remember the Civil War, the Spanish-American War appeared to represent the end of the old divisions that had led to secession. Former Union and Confederate soldiers supported a common war effort, with some from both sides donning uniforms once again.

Beginning in early 1899, Hobart suffered from fainting spells triggered by serious heart problems. He never fully recovered. In the fall of 1899, as McKinley was preparing a grand reception to honor the return of Admiral George Dewey from the Philippines, he invited the Hobarts to stay at the White House. "I can imagine no place where you will be more comfortable than here." But Hobart declined. He conceded that he must remain in Paterson and could not return to Washington either for the Dewey reception or to preside again over the Senate when it reconvened that December. This public announcement was an admission that the vice president was in "virtual retirement," with no hope of recovery. Hobart died on November 21, 1899. Arriving at the Hobart home in Paterson for the funeral, President McKinley told the family, "No one outside of this home feels this loss more deeply than I do."[107] History has remembered Garret Hobart less for his life than for his death.

---

[106] Harold U. Faulkner, *Politics, Reform and Expansion 1890-1900* (New York, 1959), p. 258; Lewis L. Gould, *The Presidency of William McKinley* (Lawrence, KY, 1980), p. 150.
[107] Magie, pp. 176, 212-17, 231; Hobart, p. 68.

THEODORE ROOSEVELT 25TH VICE PRESIDENT: 1901

Senator Thomas C. Platt of New York declared that he went to the presidential inaugural of 1901 "to see Theodore Roosevelt take the veil."[108] Roosevelt, the governor of New York, had been elected vice president the previous autumn on William McKinley's Republican ticket, and Platt looked forward to having the maverick governor in seclusion for four years. The new vice president was not entirely certain of his own prospects, stating that "it [the vice presidency] is not a steppingstone to anything except oblivion" – hardly a ringing endorsement of the nation's second highest office.[109] Yet this was the prevailing opinion about the vice-presidency at the beginning of the twentieth century. Most of Roosevelt's nearest predecessors were men of limited qualifications and interests whose functions were primarily social. Some observers hoped that this office would finally tame the firebrand Roosevelt, but if the Rough Rider's active and adventurous past was any indication, the vice-presidency was in for some changes.

In 1881, at the age of twenty-three, Roosevelt was elected to the New York state assembly as a Republican. He quickly established himself as the leader of a group of young independent-minded Republican legislators, known as the "Roosevelt Republicans," who fought to clean up New York politics by opposing the power of both the Republican state machine and the Tammany Hall Democrats of New York City. Roosevelt gained a widespread reputation for honesty, integrity, and vigor. In this second term, he was made minority leader of the assembly and in his third term collaborated often with Democratic Governor Grover Cleveland to pass reform legislation, especially civil service reform.[110]

This seemingly charmed career was sidetracked in February of 1884, when Roosevelt suffered the deaths of both his wife and his mother. He had met the beautiful Alice Lee while he was at Harvard and they had married on October 27, 1880, a handsome couple who delighted in the social life of New York. Alice became ill with Bright's Disease immediately after giving birth to their first child, also named Alice. At the same time, Martha Roosevelt lay ill

---

[108] Quoted in Irving G. Williams, *The Rise of the Vice Presidency* (Washington, D.C., 1956), p. 81.

[109] Morison, 2:1439.

[110] Ibid., pp. 159-201, 227-67; William Henry Harbaugh, *Power and Responsibility: The Life and Times of Theodore Roosevelt* (New York, 1961), pp. 27-28. Harbaugh provides the most thorough scholarly account of Roosevelt's public career.

with typhoid fever in an upstairs room. On Valentine's Day, 1884, Martha died, followed the next morning by Alice, who died in her husband's arms. The blow was tremendous, causing Theodore to lament in his diary, "The light has gone out of my life." He never spoke of Alice Lee Roosevelt again. He declined to run for reelection to the assembly, deciding instead to go west and forget his sorrows by becoming a cowboy. He purchased a ranch in the Dakota Territory and spent the text two years tending to a large herd of cattle, chasing outlaws, writing popular books about the West such as *Hunting Tips of a Ranchman* (1885), and creating an image as one of the nation's most enigmatic cowboys.[111]

Even in his attempts at seclusion, Roosevelt could not entirely escape from politics. After losing the three-way mayoral race of 1886 and spending a few years on his literary pursuits, Roosevelt held a succession of appointed posts in which he performed well and continued to enhance his public reputation. In 1897, President William McKinley appointed him assistant secretary of the navy. Roosevelt found himself in this office when the United States declared war on Spain in 1898. Never one to miss the action, Roosevelt promptly resigned his post to form a volunteer regiment of western cowboys and eastern adventurers that the press dubbed "Roosevelt's Rough Riders." The Spanish-American War did not last long, but it was long enough for the Rough Riders to ride (or march, since only Colonel Roosevelt was actually mounted) into American folklore. After the well-chronicled Battle of San Juan, Roosevelt returned to the United States as the most famous man in the nation.[112]

In the summer of 1898, the New York Republican Party was searching for a gubernatorial candidate. Roosevelt's campaign was rather simple; he promised merely to run a "clean" administration and capitalized on his popularity with the voters.

During Roosevelt's term as governor, many of his friends and admirers began once more to consider his future. As governor of New York, he naturally became a potential candidate for president. While flattered by all the support for his candidacy, Roosevelt did not relish the idea of being vice president. He worried that as vice president he "could not do anything." The more Roosevelt thought about it, the less appealing the vice-presidency

---

[111] Morris, pp. 240-45, 270-341. As chairman of the Stockman's Association, Roosevelt was automatically a deputy sheriff of Billing's County, a responsibility he took very seriously.

[112] Ibid., Chapters 16-25.

became. He continually expressed this opinion to anyone who asked, finally stating, "I would a great deal rather be anything, say professor of history, than Vice-President."

By the time the Republican National Convention opened in June in Philadelphia, it had become obvious that Roosevelt was the favorite to receive the vice-presidential nomination. When he continued to protest that he would rather be governor of New York, Lodge warned him that, if he attended the convention, his nomination was assured. But Roosevelt could not stay away; claiming that to do so would look like cowardice. Everything pointed to the vice-presidency, and Theodore Roosevelt knew how to read the signs. He did not pursue the office, but when it was thrust upon him, he accepted it. For good or ill, he was not President McKinley's running mate and he was determined to make the best of it.

Because of his lack of interest in the official duties of his new office, Roosevelt in the summer of 1901 began looking for other activities and focused on two. First, he resumed a regular speaking schedule. Vice President Roosevelt's second activity revealed his ambition. He spent considerable time lining up support for a presidential bid in 1904.

Early in September 1901, everything changed. On September 5 President McKinley, a longtime advocate of protective tariffs, delivered a major policy speech at the pan American Exposition in Buffalo, New York. The next day, September 6, the president held a public reception in the Temple of Music. At slightly after 4 p.m., a young anarchist named Leon Czolgosz walked up to the president with a gun in his right hand, hidden in a bandage. He fired two shots at the president: one bounced off a button, but the other lodged in McKinley's stomach. For a week, the president struggled to survive, but on September 14 he expired.

After paying his respects to Mrs. McKinley, Roosevelt met with the cabinet, telling them, "I wish to say that it shall be my aim to continue, absolutely unbroken, the policy of President McKinley for the peace, prosperity, and the honor of our beloved country." Roosevelt's pledge to continue McKinley's policies was not only meant to calm the nation, but was consistent with his conception of the role of the vice president.

The vice presidency led, not to oblivion, but to the White House.

CHARLES WARREN FAIRBANKS
26TH VICE PRESIDENT: 1905-1909

In the summer of 1904 Senator Charles Warren Fairbanks wanted to be president of the United States. Many in 1900 had seen him as the natural successor to his good friend President William McKinley. Now, however, it was not the fallen McKinley who occupied the White House, but Theodore Roosevelt, and the president appeared on his way to easy re-nomination at the 1904 Republican convention. When members of the Republican Old Guard suggested Fairbanks for vice president, the senator saw an opportunity for advancement. After all, the second spot had led to the presidency for Roosevelt; it might do the same for him. The vice-presidency might prove a good place from which to maneuver for the 1908 Convention, and anything could happen with the impetuous Roosevelt in the White House. As Finley Peter Dunne's fictional character Mr. Dooley speculated, "Th' way they got Sinitor Fairbanks to accipt was by showin' him a pitcher iv our gr-reat an' noble presidint thryin to jump a horse over a six-foot fence."[113] Most of all, Roosevelt's prodigious shadow seemed a natural place for a man described by friends as "as safe and popular politician" to wait for his turn in the White House.[114] If ever man seemed destined to remain in the political shadows, it was Charles Warren Fairbanks.

Fairbanks' Senate career proved competent if unspectacular. He stuck to the party line and was well respected among his colleagues. Charles Fairbanks' political fortunes changed dramatically on September 6, 1901, when President McKinley was assassinated while visiting the Pan-American Exposition in Buffalo. He lost not only a friend, but also a political patron. Although McKinley's successor, Theodore Roosevelt, promised to continue the fallen president's policies, Fairbanks' close connection to the White House was severed. Beyond these personal considerations, the nation's political environment was about to change – partly in response to Roosevelt – in ways that would leave Fairbanks in the shadows. President Roosevelt brought a new glamour to the presidency. He dominated the news and shifted the national

---

[113] James H. Madison, "Charles Warren Fairbanks and Indiana Republicanism," in Ralph D. Gray, ed., *Gentlemen From Indiana: National Party Candidates, 1836-1940* (Indianapolis, 1977), p. 184.

[114] William Henry Smith, *The Life and Speeches of Hon. Charles Warren Fairbanks* (Indianapolis, 1904), p. 7.

debate to new issues.[115] None of these changes proved helpful to Fairbanks presidential ambitions.

Still, the Old Guard could not simply be dismissed. If one of their own could not be the presidential nominee, they would choose the vice-presidential candidate. Fairbanks was the obvious choice, since conservatives thought highly of him yet he managed not to offend the party's more progressive elements. Roosevelt was far from pleased with the idea of Fairbanks for vice president. He would have preferred Representative Robert R. Hitt of Illinois, but he did not consider the vice-presidential nomination worth a fight. Fairbanks was easily placed on the 1904 Republican ticket in order to appease the Old Guard.

If the goal of constructing a national presidential ticket is to achieve a complementary balance between its two members, the Republican ticket of 1904 came close to being ideal. Roosevelt and Fairbanks differed from one another in nearly every way. The ticket offered balance both geographically, between New York and Indiana, and ideologically, from progressive to conservative. Perhaps the greatest contrast was one of personality. The vigorous and ebullient Roosevelt differed markedly from the calm and cool Fairbanks. One wag called the 1904 ticket "The Hot Tamale and the Indiana Icicle."

In an 1896 article for *Review of Reviews*, Roosevelt, while New York City police commissioner, had argued that the vice president should participate actively in a presidential administration, including attendance at cabinet meetings and consultation on all major decisions. He even posited that the vice president should be given a regular vote in the Senate.[116] Now that he was president, however, Roosevelt displayed no intention of following his own advice. He did not invite Fairbanks to participate in the cabinet and consulted the vice president about nothing of substance. Roosevelt certainly showed no inclination to support granting Fairbanks a vote in the Senate and, given Fairbanks' conservative tendencies, would probably have opposed any attempt to do so. Discussing the office abstractly turned out to be quite different from

---

[115] For the most thorough discussion of Roosevelt's presidency, see Lewis L. Gould, *The Presidency of Theodore Roosevelt* (Lawrence, KS, 1991). For a discussion of Roosevelt's vice-presidency, see "Theodore Roosevelt" in this volume.

[116] Theodore Roosevelt, "The Three Vice-Presidential Candidates and What They Represent," *American Monthly Review of Reviews* 14 (September 1896): 289-97.

dealing with a flesh-and-blood occupant. The new vice president spent much of his time presiding over the Senate.

The most famous instance of Fairbanks' effectiveness as presiding officer came in May 1908 during debate over the conference report on the Aldrich-Vreeland Emergency Currency Act. This legislation authorized the issuance of emergency currency based on state bonds, municipal bonds, and railroad bonds.

The passage of the Aldrich-Vreeland Act pleased President Roosevelt, but his vice president's other Senate rulings would not always produce such agreeable results. The Senate, especially, erected roadblocks to the president's legislative initiatives, particularly those seeking to expand the powers of the executive branch. The Hepburn bill included provisions allowing the Interstate Commerce Commission to set railroad rates, and Roosevelt pursued legislation to allow executive agencies to set maximum prices for certain commodities. While the Senate eventually agreed to the Hepburn bill with some modifications, it jealously guarded its prerogatives against what it saw as presidential encroachment.

During his vice-presidency, Fairbanks also spent considerable time trying to secure the Republican presidential nomination in 1908. Fairbanks' popularity increased somewhat after a supposed attempt on his life. While the vice president was laying the cornerstone for a new federal building in Flint, Michigan, police arrested a man in the crowd carrying a thirty-two-caliber revolver and pockets full of "socialistic literature." This incident surely evoked memories of the assassination of President McKinley. Still, no one outside the inner circle of the Republican Party seemed to pay much attention. In his effort to attract support, Fairbanks' oratory proved less than appealing. The *Nation* declared, "No public speaker can more quickly drive an audience to despair."

An even more serious problem for Fairbanks loomed in the form of opposition from Theodore Roosevelt. The president had already announced he would not run in 1908, but he intended to choose his own successor. His list clearly did not include Fairbanks. Against the power of a popular incumbent president, Fairbanks never had a chance.

After the inauguration of William Howard Taft and new Vice President James Sherman in March 1909, Fairbanks returned to Indiana to live the life of a country gentleman.

By understanding party politics, Fairbanks advanced as far as the vice-presidency. Yet, in an era dominated by the likes of Roosevelt, Wilson, Bryan, and La Follette, Fairbanks' political skills were not sufficient to allow him to escape the shadows of those men.

JAMES SCHOOLCRAFT SHERMAN
27TH VICE PRESIDENT: 1909-1912

A marble bust of James Schoolcraft Sherman has the distinction of being the only vice-presidential bust in the United States Capitol with eyeglasses. Sherman apparently had thought that no one would recognize him without his glasses. However, over time he has grown so obscure that no one recognizes him even *with* his glasses.[117] Capitol visitors often confuse him with the more famous Senator John Sherman, author of the Sherman Antitrust Act. Yet while he never authored a famous bill, "Sunny Jim" Sherman was a powerful leader in the House of Representatives, a skilled parliamentarian, and a popular presiding officer of the Senate during his vice-presidency under William Howard Taft.

While in the House, Sherman was a leader in the fight to preserve the gold standard against Populist proposals for "free silver" – by which farmers hoped to reduce their debts by fueling inflation through an expansion of the amount of money in circulation. Sherman also fought to lower the tariff. When the Republicans returned to power with the election of William McKinley as president in 1896, Sherman played a key role in passage of the Dingley Tariff that reversed Democratic efforts and restored the high protective tariff.

---

[117] Senate Curator James Ketchum provided the following information in response to the popular belief that Sherman's marble bust was damaged in the 1983 explosion that took place on the second floor of the Capitol's Senate wing, adjacent to the Sherman bust. "As Bessie Potter Vonnoh began working on the translation of her Sherman bust from plaster to marble, she discovered an imperfection near the surface of the stone. She raised her concern about its possible effect on the finished piece with the Senate Library Committee. In response, Chairman George Peabody Wetmore asked architect Thomas Hastings (of the firm of Carrere and Hastings) and sculptor James Earle Fraser to look into the matter. Both agreed that the discoloration on the right cheek was of little concern. Unfortunately, as the carving progressed, the dark spot became more apparent. There was little that could be done to minimize it and the work proceeded to completion. After the 1983 bombing of the Capitol, it was erroneously reported that the area in question, located just below Sherman's glasses, resulted from the explosion. The bust of J.S. Sherman, including his glasses, survived that bombing unscathed."

McKinley's assassination in 1901 transferred the presidency to the dynamic Theodore Roosevelt, whose strong personality stimulated a national reform movement that had grown out of a series of local responses to the human abuses of industrialism. Progressives demanded change, which conservative leaders in Congress resisted. Sherman stood with the Old Guard. "He was preeminently a standpatter and proud of it," recalled Senator Chauncey Depew. Having inherited the presidency of the New Hartford Canning Company from his father, Sherman fought progressive efforts to require accurate labeling of the weights and measures of canned jelly, catsup, corn, and other foods. He proposed a substitute amendment that required only that if a canner did label the weight and measure of the product, that such labeling must be accurate. This caused Dr. Harvey Wiley, who led the crusade for pure food and drug laws, to rename "Sunny Jim" Sherman as "Short-weight Jim."

Sherman chaired the Republican Congressional Campaign Committee during the congressional elections of 1906, raising large campaign contributions from business interests and gaining further recognition from his party's leaders.

In 1908, Sherman chaired the Republican State convention for the third time (having previously done so in 1895 and 1900). His supporters then launched a vice-presidential boom for him. President Theodore Roosevelt had announced that he would not stand for a third term, and had anointed Secretary of War William Howard Taft as his successor. Taft won the nomination and would have preferred a progressive running mate, someone of the stature of Indiana Senator Albert Beveridge or Iowa Senator Jonathan Dolliver. But House members, led by Speaker Cannon, pressed for the nomination of James Sherman. On the surface, it seemed as though Sherman won the nomination by default, after the more progressive possibilities withdrew their names form consideration.

While well-known in Washington, Sherman had little popular identification across the nation, and it is doubtful that he brought many votes to the Taft ticket. The opposition Democratic candidate was William Jennings Bryan, who had twice before lost the presidency, in 1896 and 1900. Few Republicans would have voted for Bryan regardless of who ran with Taft, but Sherman campaigned with good grace. For the third and last time, William Jennings Bryan went down to defeat as Taft and Sherman were elected.

When Taft met with Speaker Joseph Cannon in December 1908, he learned that the House Ways and Means Committee was at work on major tariff revisions. Taft favored lowering tariff rates and negotiating reciprocal trade agreements with other nations to stimulate international trade, but congressional conservatives remained committed to high tariff duties to protect American industries. House Ways and Means Committee chairman Sereno Payne eventually produced the Payne bill, which pleased Taft by its moderate tariff reductions. In the Senate, however, Finance Committee chairman Nelson Aldrich amended the tariff with massive increases in rates. Insurgent Republicans led by Wisconsin Senator Robert La Follette fought the Payne-Aldrich Tariff, but Aldrich prevailed. Never in doubt was the stance of the Senate's new presiding officer, Vice President Sherman, a lifelong high-tariff man. In the end, President Taft sided with Sherman and the protectionists and signed the bill.

The more conservative the president became, the closer he grew to his vice president. Taft found that he liked Sherman, a man who "hated shams, believed in regular party organization, and was more anxious to hold the good things established by the past than to surrender them in search for less certain benefits to be derived from radical changes in the future."

From all accounts, Sherman showed fairness, judicial temperament, and good humor in his capacity as presiding officer. Always showing his sunny disposition in public, Sherman played tough-minded, hardball politics in private. "Sherman's indictments," President Taft once complained, "are as abrupt and severe as a school master's." when progressives revolted against the Payne-Aldrich tariff, Sherman advised: "Mr. President, you can't cajole these people. You have to hit them with a club."

Senator Robert La Follette emerged as the principal challenger to Taft's re-nomination, but when the overworked and exhausted La Follette suffered a breakdown in February 1912, Theodore Roosevelt jumped into the race for the Republican nomination. In a series of bitter confrontations, Roosevelt won the popular primaries but Taft retained control of the party machinery that chose a majority of the delegates. In New York, Sherman's forces managed to gain 78 delegates for Taft, with only 12 for Roosevelt.[118] Denied the nomination, the former president walked out of the Republican convention to form the Progressive ("Bull Moose") party. Democrats meanwhile had nominated the

---

[118] Holthusen, p. 80.

progressive governor of New Jersey, Woodrow Wilson, who became the frontrunner by virtue of the Republican split. With Taft's defeat in the November elections an almost foregone conclusion, the Republican convention re-nominated Sherman with little fuss or attention. He became the first sitting vice president to be re-nominated since John C. Calhoun, eighty years earlier. The Democratic candidate, Woodrow Wilson, won the presidency with 435 electoral votes; the Progressive candidate, Theodore Roosevelt, took second place with 88 electoral votes; and Taft came in a dismal third, with only the 8 electoral votes of Vermont and Utah. In January, the Republican National Committee named another New Yorker, Columbia University president Nicholas Butler, to fill out the Republican ticket for purposes of receiving electoral votes, which were counted on February 12, 1913. Taft's reelection campaign remains one of the worst defeats ever suffered by a Republican presidential candidate (in 1936, Alf Landon tied Taft by winning only 8 electoral votes).[119]

James Schoolcraft Sherman quickly disappeared from public memory. He remained the least-remembered twentieth-century vice president until 1974, when he made an unexpected reappearance in E.L. Doctorow's best-selling novel *Ragtime*. Sherman simply served as the novelist's metaphor of an unhealthy and unresponsive political system. Although perhaps better than total obscurity, it was not the way "Sunny Jim" would have wanted to be remembered.

THOMAS R. MARSHALL 28TH VICE PRESIDENT: 1913-1921

Vice President Thomas R. Marshall, who served two terms with President Woodrow Wilson from 1913 to 1921, claimed that most of the "nameless, unremembered" jobs assigned to him had been concocted essentially to keep vice presidents from doing any harm to their administrations. One of these chores, according to Marshall, was that of regent of the Smithsonian Institution. The vice president recalled that at his first board meeting the other regents, including the chief justice of the United States and the inventor Alexander Graham Bell, discussed funding an expedition to Guatemala to excavate for traces of prehistoric man. With the breezy manner of a self-described "light-hearted Hoosier," Marshall asked if the Smithsonian had ever

---

[119] *New York Times*, November 3, 1912, January 5, 1913.

considered excavating in Washington, D.C. Judging from the specimens walking about on the street, he said, they would not have to dig far below the capital to discover prehistoric man. "And then the utter uselessness and frivolity of the vice-presidency was disclosed," Marshall confessed, "for not a man smiled. It was a year before I had courage to open my mouth again."[120]

This typically self-deprecating story revealed much about Marshall's lamentable vice-presidency. His feelings of inadequacy in both himself and the position he held were reflected again in his reaction to an invitation from President Wilson to attend cabinet meetings. Vice President Marshall stopped going after a single session. When asked why, he replied that he realized "he would not be listened to and hence would be unable to make any contribution." Marshall similarly attended only one meeting of the Senate Democratic Caucus. "I do not blame proud parents for wishing that their sons might be President of the United States," he later said. "But if I sought a blessing for a boy I would not pray that he become Vice-President."[121]

Woodrow Wilson, a supremely self-confident intellectual, regarded Marshall as a "small-caliber man" and had not wanted him on his ticket in 1912.[122] During their eight years together, Wilson undoubtedly made Marshall feel uncomfortable. The editor William Allen White once described presenting a proposal to Wilson at the White House. Wilson "parried and countered quickly, as one who had heard the argument I would present and was punctiliously impatient. He presented another aspect of the case and outtalked me, agreeing in nothing. I could not tell how much he assimilated."[123] For a more insecure man like Marshall, such a response must have been excruciating. Convinced that the president and other high-ranking officials did not take him seriously enough to listen to him, Marshall learned not to speak, not to attend meetings, and not to offer suggestions. He became the epitome of the vice president as non-entity. But this condition moved from comedy to tragedy when President Wilson suffered a paralytic stroke in 1919. Faced with

---

[120] Thomas R. Marshall, *Recollections of Thomas R. Marshall, Vice-President and Hoosier Philosopher: A Hoosier Salad* (Indianapolis, 1925), pp. 16-18.

[121] Ray Stannard Baker, *Woodrow Wilson, Life and Letters* (Garden City, N.Y., 1931), 4:104-9; and Daniel C. Roper, *Fifty Years of Public Life* (Durham, NC, 1941); John E. Brown, "Woodrow Wilson's Vice President: Thomas R. Marshall and the Wilson Administration, 1913-1921" (Ph.D. dissertation, Ball State University, 1970), p. 216.

[122] Charles M. Thomas, *Thomas Riley Marshall, Hoosier Statesman* (Oxford, OH, 1939), p. 129.

[123] William Allen White, *The Autobiography of William Allen White* (New York, 1946), pp. 615-16.

the crisis of having to determine whether the president was able to fulfill the duties of his office, Marshall failed miserably.

Thomas R. Marshall went to Washington "with the feeling that the American people might have made a mistake in setting me down in the company of all the wise men in the land." His job as vice president required him to preside over the Senate, but other than delivering his gubernatorial messages to the Indiana legislature, Marshall had no legislative experience. He assumed that as presiding officer of the Senate he had some authority, but it did not take him long to discover "that the Senate was not only a self-governing body but that it was a quite willful set of men, who had not the slightest hesitancy in overruling a presiding officer."

A slight bespectacled man, with his hat pushed back on his head, a pipe or cigar always ready in his hand, Marshall knew that he "was too small to look dignified in a Prince Albert coat," and so he continued his ordinary manner of dress. "He is calm and serene and small; mild, quiet, simple and old-fashioned," as one Indiana writer described him. "His hair is gray and so is his mustache. His clothes are gray and so is his tie. He has a cigar tucked beneath the mustache and his gray fedora had shades his gray eyes." Another observer characterized Marshall's voice as "musical, pleasant in tone, and …sufficient for stump-speaking out of doors, although you wouldn't think it to hear its soft notes in conversation."[124]

Serving under a vigorous and innovative president, Marshall had difficulty determining his own role. It was clear that the president intended to be his own lobbyist on Capitol Hill and had no particular use for his vice president. Marshall quickly ascertained that he was "of no importance to the administration beyond the duty of being loyal to it and ready, at any time, to act as a sort of pinch hitter; that is, when everybody else on the team had failed, I was to be given a chance."

Although both men had served as Democratic governors and both were Calvinist Presbyterians, Wilson and Marshall in fact had little in common. Even in the Senate, Marshall was overshadowed by his two fellow Indianans, both progressive Democrats.

In 1916, the Democratic convention re-nominated Wilson and Marshall. Marshall's second term proved difficult and stressful. In April 1917, the United States entered the First World War, joining the allied forces against

---

[124] Ibid., p. 233; Brown, pp. 50-51.

Germany. On December 4, 1918, President Wilson sailed for France to negotiate the peace treaty. Except for the few days between February 24 and March 5, 1919, Wilson remained out of the country until July, after the Treaty of Versailles had been signed. During Wilson's unprecedented long absences from the United States, he designated Vice President Marshall to preside over cabinet meetings in his place. The request startled Marshall, but he complied gamely. Marshall presided only briefly over the cabinet, withdrawing after a few sessions on the grounds that the vice president could not maintain a confidential relationship with both the executive and legislative branches. Still, he had established the precedent of presiding over the cabinet during the president's absence, making it particularly difficult to understand why he failed to carry out that same duty in October 1919, after Wilson suffered a paralytic stroke.

It was Secretary of State Robert Lansing who determined to call cabinet meetings in the president's absence. Without the participation of either the president or vice president, the cabinet met regularly between October 1919 and February 1920, presided over by Secretary of State Lansing, or in his absence, Secretary of Treasury Carter Glass. When Wilson recovered sufficiently, he fired Lansing for attempting to "oust" him from office by calling these meetings. Wilson, who was never himself after his stroke, argued that these meetings held no purpose since no cabinet decisions could be made without the president. Yet Wilson himself had sanctioned the cabinet meetings over which Marshall had presided a year earlier. If nothing else, for the cabinet to hold regular meetings at least assured the American public that their government continued to function.

The Constitution declares that the vice president could assume the duties of president in case of the president's "Inability to discharge the Powers and Duties of the said Office," but until the Twenty-fifth Amendment was adopted in 1967, the Constitution said absolutely nothing about how he should do it.[125] Marshall was clearly in a difficult situation. As editor Henry L. Stoddard observed, "Wilson's resentment of Lansing's activities is proof that Vice President Marshall would have had to lay siege to the White House, had he assumed the Presidency."

Marshall himself told the story of riding on a train behind a man and a woman who were discussing the news that President Wilson had removed

Secretary of State Lansing for holding cabinet meetings. "Why what else could Mr. Lansing have done?" the woman asked. "Here the President is sick. A lot of big questions had to be talked over and there was the Vice President, who doesn't amount to anything. The only thing Mr. Lansing could do, I tell you, was to call these Cabinet meetings, and I think he did the right thing." Said Marshall, "There you have it in a nutshell. The woman was right. I don't amount to anything."[126]

Although Thomas Marshall publicly hinted that he would accept the Democratic nomination for president in 1920, few delegates outside of Indiana cast any votes for him.

CALVIN COOLIDGE 29ᵀᴴ VICE PRESIDENT: 1921-1923

Calvin Coolidge came to the vice presidency from the governorship of Massachusetts, but he was at heart a Vermonter. Born in Vermont on the Fourth of July 1872, he died in Vermont sixty-one years later, on January 5, 1933. During the years between, he lived most of his adult life in Massachusetts and worked out of the statehouse in Boston but never identified with Back Bay society. "I come from Boston," a lady once identified herself to him when he was president. "Yes, and you'll never get over it," Coolidge replied dryly. One of Coolidge's first biographers, Claude Fuess, identified him as the archetypical Yankee, "with his wiry, nervous body, his laconic speech, his thrift, his industry, his conservative distrust of foreigners and innovations, and his native dignity." This dour, taciturn man served eight years as vice president and president during the "Roaring Twenties," an era remembered for its speakeasies, flappers, and anything-goes attitudes. Calvin Coolidge, as journalist William Allen White aptly recorded, was "A Puritan in Babylon."[127]

"Silent Cal" became famous for his words. In a telegram to AFL President Samuel Gompers, Coolidge asserted, "There is no right to strike against the public safety of anybody, anywhere, any time." At a time when the nation was rocked by a series of often-violent postwar labor disputes, many citizens

[125] See Birch Bayh, *One Heartbeat Away: Presidential Disability and Succession* (Indianapolis, 1968).
[126] Brown, pp. 418-19.
[127] Claude M. Fuess, *Calvin Coolidge: The Man from Vermont* (Boston, 1940), p. 5; William Allen White, *A Puritan in Babylon: The Story of Calvin Coolidge* (New York, 1938).

welcomed this message. Coolidge became the "law and order" governor. His photograph appeared on the front pages of newspapers nationwide, and thousands of telegrams and letters poured in to congratulate him. There was talk of running Calvin Coolidge for president in 1920.

New York Times correspondent Charles Willis Thompson was among the many journalists curious about this new phenomenon. Thompson noted that Coolidge began making political speeches outside of Massachusetts but not in such likely places as Chicago and New York. Instead, Coolidge went to Oregon and to the Rocky Mountain states, and his speeches were always on nonpolitical themes. "Each one of these nonpolitical speeches had in it that quality of arrest; there was something in it, unpretentious as it was as a whole, that made you stop and think," Thompson observed. "There was nothing spectacular about him yet, or ever." The 1920 Republican convention opened in Chicago with many candidates and no clear frontrunner. They were determined to name someone who would reduce the powers of the presidency, which they believed had expanded disproportionately during the administrations of Theodore Roosevelt and Woodrow Wilson. To this end, they chose one of their most pliable colleagues, Ohio Senator Warren G. Harding, as the Republican presidential nominee.

Harding had been far from a leading contender among the delegates, who nominated him with out much enthusiasm. Seeking to balance the conservative Harding, and hoping to make it an all-senatorial ticket, the senators first offered the vice-presidential nomination to California Senator Hiram Johnson, who turned it down. They next went to progressive Senator Irvine Lenroot of Wisconsin. When Illinois Senator Medill McCormick stepped to the podium to nominate Lenroot, a delegate from Portland, Oregon, former Judge Wallace McCamant, called out loudly, "Coolidge! Coolidge! Other delegates took up the cry. When Senator McCormick finished his address, McCamant leaped on a chair among the Oregon delegation and nominated Governor Calvin Coolidge of Massachusetts for vice president. Showing enthusiasm for the first time, the delegates demonstrated spontaneously in Coolidge's behalf. Lenroot would be "just one too many Senators on the presidential ticket," a reported observed. Delegates for other candidates who felt they had been denied their choice for the top spot were determined to have a voice in the second place. They voted 674 for Coolidge to 146 for Lenroot.

It had been perhaps the most unusual and independent vice-presidential nomination in American political history. Where parties normally balance, both Harding and Coolidge were unabashed conservatives and comprised the most conservative ticket since the party had gone down to disastrous defeat in 1912. But in 1920 that proved to be exactly what the nation wanted, and in November the Harding-Coolidge ticket overwhelmed the Democratic ticket of James M. Cox and Franklin D. Roosevelt. At his inauguration as vice president, Calvin Coolidge took satisfaction that "the same thing for which I had worked in Massachusetts had been accomplished in the nation. The radicalism which had tinged our whole political and economic life from soon after 199 to the World War period was passed."

"Presiding over the Senate was fascinating to me," Coolidge later wrote. Although the Senate's methods at first seemed peculiar, he soon became familiar with them and suggested that they were "the best method of conducting its business.

Coolidge's most controversial moment as vice president came in July 1921. Midwestern progressive Republicans were seeking federal relief for farmers, whose sales and purchasing power had collapsed after the war. Senator George Norris of Nebraska introduced a bill that would make it easier to market American farm products overseas. The Harding Administration countered with a bill sponsored by Minnesota Senator Frank Kellogg to make domestic marketing of farm goods easier. Norris had asked Coolidge, as presiding officer, to recognize Senator Joseph E. Ransdell, a Louisiana Democrat, first. Coolidge had agreed, but then he left the chair and asked Charles Curtis of Kansas, a tough-minded partisan senator, to preside in his place. When Ransdell stood and sought recognition, Curtis ignored him and instead called upon Kellogg, who in fact was still in his seat and had not even risen to seek recognition. After the ensuing hubbub, as Kellogg claimed the floor, Coolidge reentered the chamber and once again presided. Progressive Republicans and Democrats long remembered this maneuver and never fully trusted Coolidge again.

Coolidge joined the cabinet meetings, becoming the first vice president to do so on a regular basis. Coolidge believed that, although the vice president could probably offer little insight about the Senate, and virtually nothing about the House, a vice president needed to be fully informed of what was going on in case he should become president.

The Harding administration meanwhile had become mired in scandal. The Senate had launched an investigation of improper leasing of naval oil reserves at Teapot Dome in Wyoming. There were also indications of scandals brewing in the Veterans Administration and the Department of Justice. Whether Harding would be reelected, whether he would keep Coolidge on the ticket, and whether the ticket could be reelected in the face of these scandals were all unanswerable questions in the summer of 1923, when a dispirited Harding traveled to Alaska and the Pacific Coast.

Vice President Coolidge was on vacation at his father's home in Plymouth, Vermont, when on the night of August 2, 1923, he was awakened by his father calling his name. "I noticed that his voice trembled. As the only time I had ever observed that before were when death had visited the family, I knew that something of the gravest nature had occurred," Coolidge recorded. Colonel John Coolidge informed his son that a telegram had arrived announcing that President Harding had died in San Francisco. As Calvin Coolidge noted, his father "was the first to address me as President of the United States. It was the culmination of the lifelong desire of a father for the success of his son."

After his unsatisfying years as vice president, Coolidge became a surprisingly popular president, easily winning reelection in 1924. Correspondent Charles Willis Thompson, a keen observer of presidents during the first decades of this century, believed that the nation found psychological relief in Coolidge after the high-minded oratory of Wilson and the bombast of Harding.

Coolidge was never an innovative or active president. He was largely uninterested in foreign policy. Embracing a laissez-faire philosophy opposed to government intervention, he had no bold domestic programs but carried on the policies begun under Harding. Calvin Coolidge never made any pretensions to greatness. "It is a great advantage to a President and a major source of safety to the country, for him to know that he is not a great man," he recorded in his *Autobiography*. That seems the most fitting epitaph for the man.[128]

---

[128] Coolidge, p. 173.

CHARLES G. DAWES 30TH VICE PRESIDENT: 1925-1929

It is ironic that "Silent Cal" Coolidge should have a vice president as garrulous as Charles Gates Dawes. A man of action as well as of blunt words, "Hell'n Maria" Dawes (the favorite expression by which he was known) was in so many ways the opposite of President Coolidge that the two men were never able to establish a working relationship. The president probably never forgave his vice president for stealing attention from him at their inaugural ceremonies, nor did he ever forget that Dawes was responsible for one of his most embarrassing defeats in the Senate. As a result, although Dawes was one of the most notable and able men to occupy the vice-presidency, his tenure was not a satisfying or productive one, nor did it stand as a model for others to follow.

Charles Dawes was not Calvin Coolidge's choice for a running mate. It would have taken a far more self-confident president to want a vice president with a longer and more distinguished career than his own. Dawes had been a prominent official in the McKinley administration when Coolidge was still a city council member in Northampton, Massachusetts. Dawes became a highly decorated military officer during the First World War, was the president of a prestigious financial institution, was the first director of the Bureau of the Budget, and devised the "Dawes Plan" to salvage Europe's postwar economy, for which he received the Nobel Peace Prize. Dawes had a keen concern for foreign affairs, in which Coolidge showed little interest. As an activist in domestic policy, Dawes convinced the Senate to pass the McNary-Haugen farm relief bill; Coolidge vetoed the bill. Dawes was a problem solver, Coolidge a problem avoider. The 1920s might have been a very different decade if the Republican ticket in 1924 had been Dawes-Coolidge rather than Coolidge-Dawes.

When the United States entered the First World War in 1917, Dawes at age fifty-two received his commission as a major in the 17th Railway Engineers, bound for France, and, just as Hoover predicted, he was soon a lieutenant colonel. Dawes rose to the rank of brigadier general. When the Allied command was unified, General Dawes became the U.S. member of the Military Board of Allied Supply. While representing the United States Army in conferences and other Allied armies and governments, Dawes particularly admired men of action rather than those who simply talked. "Action, then, is everything – words nothing except as they lead immediately to it," he commented, adding, "I came out of the war a postgraduate in emergency conferences." After the Armistice in 1918, he remained in Europe to oversee the disposition of surplus military property. In 1919 he resigned his commission and returned to the United States. His wartime experiences in negotiating and coordinating efforts with his Allied counterparts left him an internationalist in outlook, advocating ratification of the Treaty of Versailles and United States membership in the League of Nations. After the war, everyone called him "General Dawes," despite his protests to the contrary.[129]

In 1923, the economy of Germany was deteriorated drastically. Since Germany was unable to repay its war debts, France sent troops to occupy the industrial Ruhr valley. President Harding appointed Dawes to head a commission to study and solve the German financial problem. The "Dawes Plan" offered ways to stabilize the German currency, balance its budget, and reorganize its Reichbank, but the plan postponed action on the most difficult issue of delaying and reducing the German war reparations. Nevertheless, the "Dawes Plan" was recognized as a significant enough contribution to world peace to win Dawes the 1925 Nobel Peace Prize, which he shared with his British counterpart, Sir Austen Chamberlain. Dawes donated his share of the prize money to the Walter Hines Page School of International Relations at John Hopkins University.

At the Republican convention in 1924, Calvin Coolidge was nominated without significant opposition. Coolidge and Dawes were overwhelmingly elected in 1924, winning more votes than the Democratic and Progressive candidates combined. "When Coolidge was elected President the world desired tranquility," Dawes noted in his journal, " – a reaction of its peoples from the excesses of war."[130] But tranquility was not Charles Dawes' style.

At his swearing-in in the Senate chamber in March 1925, Dawes was called upon to deliver a brief inaugural address, a tradition that dated back to John Adams in 1789. What the audience heard, however, was far from traditional. As the Senate's new presiding officer, Dawes addressed himself to "methods of effective procedure," rather than any particular policies or programs. He then launched into an attack on the Senate rules, "which, in their present form, place power in the hands of individuals to an extent, at times, subversive of the fundamental principles of free representative government." The rules of the Senate, he declared, ran contrary to the principles of

---

[129] Leach, p. 149.

constitutional government, and under these rules "the rights of the Nation and of the American people have been overlooked."[131]

Dawes focused his attack on filibusters, which at that time were being carried out most frequently by the small band of progressive Republicans, such as Robert La Follette, Sr., and George Norris, who held the balance of power in the Senate. Dawes declared that Rule 22, which required a two-thirds majority of those present and voting to shut off debate, "at times enables Senators to consume in oratory those last precious minutes of a session needed for momentous decisions," thus placing great power in the hands of the minority of senators. He concluded by appealing to senators' consciences and patriotism in correcting these defects in their rules.[132]

Since Dawes had not given advance copies of the speech to the press or anyone else, no one had anticipated his diatribe. In the audience, President Calvin Coolidge attempted indifference, but could not hide his discomfort. Dawes had managed to upstage the president's own inaugural address. As the senators proceeded to the inaugural platform, they talked of nothing else but their anger over Dawes' effrontery, making Coolidge's address anticlimactic. Most senators were less than receptive to Dawes' advice.

After upstaging the president on inaugural day, Dawes compounded his error by writing to inform Coolidge that he did not think the vice president should attend cabinet meetings. President Harding had invited Coolidge to cabinet meetings on a regular basis, but Dawes did not believe that Harding's action should necessarily set a precedent for future presidents. He took the initiative by declining even before Coolidge had offered him an invitation. "This was done to relieve him – if he shared my views – any embarrassment, if he desired to carry them out," Dawes later explained, "notwithstanding the fact that he had accepted Harding's invitation." Dawes dismissed suggestions by the "busy-bodies and mischief-makers" in Washington, who imagined "unpleasant relations between Coolidge and myself." What Coolidge thought is less certain. In his *Autobiography*, Coolidge counted his experiences in the cabinet as being "of supreme value" to him when he became president and suggested that the vice president should be invited to sit with the cabinet, if he was "a man of discretion and character so that he can be relied upon to act as a

---

[130] Dawes, *Notes as Vice President*, p. 32.
[131] McCoy, pp. 264-65; U.S., Congress, Senate, *Congressional Record*, 69th Cong., special sess., p. 3.
[132] Ibid., pp. 3-4.

subordinate in that position." The implication was that Dawes did not fit that description. In addition, Coolidge never mentioned Dawes by name in his memoirs.[133]

Rather than cease his criticism, Dawes continued to seek public forums to denounce the Senate filibuster. During the summer recess in 1925, he toured the country addressing public meetings on the subject. He pointed out that filibusters flourished during the short sessions of Congress, held between December and March following each congressional election, and that these protected debates tied up critical appropriations bills until the majority would agree to fund some individual senator's pet project. Dawes' campaign stimulated a national debate on the Senate rules. Although the Senate did not change its rules during his vice-presidency, Dawes noted with satisfaction that it invoked cloture more frequently than ever before. After 1917, when the cloture rule was first adopted, the Senate had voted to cut off debate on the Versailles Treaty in 1919 but failed to invoke cloture on tariff legislation in 1921 and 1922. During the Sixty-ninth Congress, which ran from 1925 to 1927, the Senate cast seven votes on cloture, and three times gained the two-thirds majority sufficient to cut off filibusters. Not until the Ninety-third Congress, from 1973 to 1975, after a rules change had reduced the majority needed to vote cloture from two-thirds to three-fifths of the members, did the Senate equal and surpass that number of successful cloture votes.

As a man of action, Charles Dawes found the job of presiding over Senate debates "at times rather irksome." He felt more comfortable in executive and administrative positions with "specific objectives and well-defined authority and responsibilities." He preferred clear statements of fact to speeches that appealed to prejudice or emotion. As presiding officer, he enjoyed making decisions about rulings from the chair and took some pride in the fact that the Senate had never overturned one of his decisions.

In 1927, President Coolidge stunned the nation with his announcement that he did not choose to run for reelection the following year. Although pundits debated whether Coolidge wanted to accept a draft, his announcement opened a spirited campaign for the Republican presidential nomination. Although Dawes was frequently mentioned for the presidency, he announced that he was not a candidate.

---

[133] Dawes, *Notes as Vice President*, pp. 33-34; Calvin Coolidge, *The Autobiography of Calvin Coolidge* (New York, 1929), pp. 163-64.

As Dawes' term of office approached its end, a senator told him how much the members of the Senate thought of him, adding "but the Senate got very tired of you at the beginning of your service." Dawes replied, "I should hate to think that the Senate was as tired of me at the beginning of my service as I am of the Senate at the end."[134]

Historians have concluded that if Dawes was not really a leader, he acted like one. As vice president, he would not accept direction from the president, and whenever his views did coincide with Coolidge's his lobbying on behalf of administration measures was more likely to hurt rather than help. Dawes' forthrightness and tactlessness incurred the anger of many senators. Although his "bull-like integrity" won Dawes recognition as an outstanding vice president, that quality antagonized the Coolidge Administration more than aiding it. As for Dawes, he believed that the vice-presidency "is largely what the man in it makes it." And for his part, he made the most of it.[135]

CHARLES CURTIS 31ST VICE PRESIDENT: 1929-1933

In the spring of 1932, George and Ira Gershwin's Broadway musical, "Of Thee I Sing," spoofed Washington politics, including a vice president named Alexander Throttlebottom, who could get inside the White House only on public tours. The tour guide, who failed to recognize Throttlebottom, at one point, engaged him in a discussion of the vice-presidency:

Guide: Well, how did he come to be Vice President?
Throttlebottom: Well, they put a lot of names in a hat, and he lost.
Guide: What does he do all the time?
Throttlebottom: Well, he sits in the park and feeds the peanuts to the pigeons and the squirrels, and then he takes walks, and goes to the movies. Last week, he tried to join the library, but he needed two references, so he couldn't get in.[136]

Audiences laughed heartily at these lines, in part because they could easily identify the hapless Throttlebottom with the incumbent vice president, Charles

---

[134] Dawes, *Notes as Vice President*, p. 255.
[135] McCoy, p. 247; Dawes, *Notes as Vice President*, p. 4.

Curtis. Curtis was never close to President Herbert Hoover and played no significant role in his administration. Despite Curtis' many years of experience as a member of the House and Senate and as Senate majority leader, his counsel was rarely sought on legislative matters. His chief notoriety as vice president came as a result of a messy social squabble over protocol, which only made him appear ridiculous. Many Republicans hoped to dump Curtis from the ticket when Hoover ran for reelection. Given Curtis' Horatio Alger-style rise in life, and his long and successful career in Congress, how did he become such a Throttlebottom as vice president?

When Curtis first came to Washington, Democrats firmly controlled the federal government. Grover Cleveland had just been elected to his second term as president, and in the House Democrats held 218 seats, Republicans 124, and the Populists 14. Then in 1893 a severe economic depression dramatically reversed party fortunes. Campaigning against the Democrats as the party of the "empty dinner pail," Republicans won 254 seats in the next Congress, leaving the Democrats with 93 and the Populists with 10. Tom Reed, who had resumed the speakership with the return of a Republican majority, trusted Curtis' political judgment. According to an often-repeated story, Curtis once entered Speaker Reed's office and found a group of Republicans discussing the restoration of the gold standard. "Indian, what would you do about this?" Reed asked. Curtis suggested taking the matter out of the hands of the standing committees that had been dealing with it, since it was apparent they would never agree. Instead, he recommended appointing a special committee to write a new bill. Reed liked the idea so much that he appointed Curtis as a member of the special committee that drafted the Gold Standard Act of 1900.[137]

Curtis devoted most of his attention to his service on the Committee on Indian Affairs, where he drafted the "Curtis Act" in 1898. Entitled "An Act for Protection of the People of the Indian Territory and for Other Purposes," the Curtis Act actually overturned many treaty rights by allocating federal lands, abolishing tribal courts, and giving the Interior Department control over mineral leases on Indian lands. Having reinstated his name on the Kaw tribal rolls in 1889, Curtis was able, through his position on the House Indian Affairs Committee, to calculate the benefits he might receive from

---

[136] Quoted in Chalmers Roberts, *First Rough Draft: A Journalists' Journal of Our Times* (New York, 1973), p. 268.

[137] Seitz, pp. 161-62; Ewy, p. 23.

government allotments to his tribe. In 1902, he drafted the Kaw Allotment Act under which he and his children received fee simple title to Kaw land in Oklahoma.[138]

The state legislature elected Charles Curtis senator on January 23, 1907. In 1909, Curtis played an influential role in the passage of the Payne-Aldrich Tariff, which raised rates so high that it helped split the Republican party into warring conservative and progressive factions. Two years later, that split claimed Curtis as a victim, when he was defeated for re-nomination by a progressive Republican – who in turn was defeated by a Democrat.[139]

As a result of the ratification of the Seventeenth Amendment, the first direct popular elections of senators were held in 1914. Progressives were confident that the people would support their candidates, but with an economic recession at home and war in Europe, voters nationwide instead turned to conservative candidates. After defeating the progressive incumbent Joseph Bristow for the Republican Senate nomination, Charles Curtis went on to defeat both a Democratic and a Progressive Party opponent that November.[140]

Curtis returned to the Senate in 1915 as a symbol of the rewards of party regularity and the defeat of insurgency. In 1923, Curtis became chairman of the Senate Rules Committee, and two years later he succeeded Lodge as majority leader – becoming the first Republican to hold the official title of party floor leader.

Curtis had harbored presidential ambitions for some time. In 1924 he had been widely mentioned as a vice-presidential candidate, but his wife, Anna, was seriously ill at the time. His sister Dolly volunteered to stay with her, so that Curtis could attend the convention and improve his chances for the vice-presidential nomination. "Dolly," he replied, "I would not leave Anna now to be President of the United States, and certainly not for the Vice Presidency." (Anna Curtis died on June 29, 1924.) In 1927 President Coolidge jolted the nation by announcing that he did not choose to run in 1928. Potential candidates and the press speculated endlessly about what Coolidge meant – whether he expected the convention to deadlock and then draft him or whether he would not run under any circumstances. Curtis assumed that Coolidge was

---

[138] Unrau, *Mixed-Bloods and Tribal Dissolution*, pp. 119-23; Unrau, "The Mixed-Blood Connection," p. 159.

[139] Ibid., pp. 27, 295.

[140] Ewy, pp. 27-29.

out of the race and felt assured that Coolidge favored him for president. Even Commerce Secretary Herbert Hoover privately conceded that Curtis "was a natural selection for Mr. Coolidge's type of mind."

Hoover was the frontrunner, but the farm states had remained strongly opposed to him ever since his service as "Food Czar" during the First World War, as well as because he opposed the McNary-Haugen bills. Curtis and Hoover had never been close. Recalling that Hoover had campaigned for Democratic candidates in 1918, Curtis had tried to prevent President Harding from appointing Hoover to the cabinet. Hoover saw Curtis as one of a half-dozen senators who were trying to stop his nomination by heaping attacks on him.

After announcing for president, Curtis made no speeches and continued to devote his attention to his functions as Senate majority leader. Not until Curtis reached the convention in Kansas City did he speak out against Hoover. He warned that the Republicans could not afford to nominate a candidate who would place the party "on the defensive from the day he is named." Despite caravans of farmers who protested against Hoover, the commerce secretary easily won the Republican nomination on the first ballot.[141]

To balance the ticket, Republicans sought a farm-state man for vice president and chose Charles Curtis of Kansas. Insisting that he had never sought the vice-presidency, Curtis agreed to run because of his loyalty to the party. Reporters viewed the choice of Curtis as "the perfect touch of irony" for the convention, given his earlier opposition to Hoover.

The Hoover-Curtis ticket rode to victory that November over the Democratic ticket of Alfred Smith and Joseph T. Robinson. Each of the vice-presidential candidates served as his party's floor leader in the Senate, and, despite their political differences, the two were known as "chums." Curtis was celebrated as a "stand patter," the most regular of Republicans, and yet a man who could always bargain with his party's progressives and with senators from across the center aisle. Newspapers claimed that Curtis knew the Senate rules better than any other senator and declared him "the most competent man in Congress to look after the legislative program of the administration."

This was not to be. Hoover and Curtis remained alienated after the strains of campaigning against each other for the nomination. Since their ticket had been a marriage of convenience, there was little love to lose over the next four

---

[141] *New York Times*, February 3, April 26 and June 11-15, 1928; Ewy, pp. 230-31.

years. Neither man mentioned the other in his inaugural address, and except for formal occasions they seem to have had little to do with each other as possible. A politico not identified with issues or ideas, Curtis could never measure up to Hoover's standards and never became an inside player. Although Curtis attended some cabinet meetings, his advice was neither sought nor followed. He spend his vice-presidency presiding over the Senate, and on a few occasions casting tie-breaking votes.

Curtis enjoyed the status of the vice-presidency and made much of his rise "from Kaw tepee to Capitol." As the first American of Indian ancestry to reach high office, he decorated his office with Native American artifacts and posed for pictures wearing Indian headdresses. But the press who covered him noted that Charles Curtis had changed in many ways, both subtle and conspicuous. As a senator, he had always been a "placid, humble, unchanging, decent fellow," but when he began to harbor presidential ambitions "his humility turned inside out." Curtis grew pompous, demanding that past intimates address him as the vice president of the Unites States and giving the impression that he felt that he, rather than Herbert Hoover, should be occupying the White House. Perhaps sensing that resentment, the Hoover White House never trusted Curtis as a legislative lieutenant.

When the stock market crashed in 1929, the nation began to slip into the worst economic depression in its history. At a moment when people wanted positive action from their political leaders, poor Curtis became embarrassingly embroiled in a "tempest in a teapot." His sister Dolly openly feuded with Alice Roosevelt Longworth, the daughter of Theodore Roosevelt and wife of House Speaker Nicholas Longworth, over their relative positions in protocol. "Princess Alice" admitted making a "little mischief" over the affair. After Curtis' wife died, Dolly had invited him to live at her Washington home and had acted as his official hostess. Dolly Gann asserted that as hostess for the vice president she should be seated ahead of the congressional and diplomatic wives at Washington dinners. "At that there was a cackle of excited discussion about the propriety of designating any one not a wife to hold the rank of one," observed Alice Longworth. Alice raised the issue with her husband Nick, who disapproved of Dolly Gann's pretensions and used the controversy as an excuse to avoid going to Prohibition-era "dry" dinner parties that he hated to attend. All this caused a "torrent of newspaper publicity," predominantly negative.

Bad press dogged Curtis and he assumed the public image of a Throttlebottom, especially as a result of his panicky response to the bonus marchers of 1932. World War I veterans had marched on Washington to demand that Congress pass legislation enabling them to receive early payment of their promised bonus for wartime service. As a senator, Curtis had sponsored an earlier bonus bill and, although he himself had never served in the military, he frequently cited his father's Civil War service in seeking veterans' support for his campaigns. But when the marchers camped around Washington and paraded to the Capitol, Curtis urged President Hoover to call out the troops. The president, however, tried to keep calm and maintain the peace.[142]

As the depression worsened and the presidential election approached, many Republicans talked of dumping Curtis from the ticket in favor of a stronger candidate who might help Hoover's chance of reelection. Curtis himself recognized his vulnerability and talked of running for the Senate seat from Kansas instead. But with his sister Dolly rallying support among the delegates, Curtis was re-nominated on the Hoover ticket to face Franklin D. Roosevelt and John Nance Garner. In the depth of the depression, the Hoover-Curtis campaign never stood a chance. Hecklers challenged Curtis when he spoke. Why had he not fed the veterans in Washington? they yelled at one stop. "I've fed more than you have, you dirty cowards!" Curtis shouted back at the crowd. "I'm not afraid of you!" The crowd chanted "Hurrah for Roosevelt!"[143]

A landslide defeat in November 1932 retired Charles Curtis from a political career that had begun almost fifty years earlier when he ran for Shawnee County district attorney. A party regular – "one-eighth Kaw Indian and a one-hundred percent Republican" as he liked to tell audiences – he had been yoked to one of the most intellectual and least political of all American

---

[142] Daniel J. Lisio, *The President and Protest: Hoover, Conspiracy, and The Bonus Riot* (Columbia, MO, 1974), p. 218.
[143] Williams, p. 147; Ewy, pp. 51-52; Lisio, p. 244.

presidents, and the incompatibility of the team made his vice-presidency a dismal failure.[144]

---

[144] Unrau, Mixed-Bloods and Tribal Dissolution, p. 112.

INDEX

X